FOUND MONEY

the chief executive press

FOUND MONEY

AL EHRBAR

whittle direct books

Photographs: J. Burgess Winter and Harry R.Clark by Bebe O'Brien,
courtesy of Magma Copper Company, page 8; Jon H. Simpson by Melanie Eve
Barocas, page 40; Robert W. Galvin by Michael L. Abramson/Woodfin Camp,
page 48; Jack F. Reichert by Katherine Lambert, page 67.

The Chief Executive Press: Dorothy Foltz-Gray, Senior Editor;
Ken Smith, Design Director; Evelyn Ellis, Art Director

Library of Congress Catalog Card Number: 93-60053
Ehrbar, Al
Found Money
ISBN 1-879736-12-8
ISSN 1060-8923

the chief executive press

The Chief Executive Press presents original short books by distinguished authors on subjects of special importance to the topmost executives of the world's major businesses.

The series is edited and published by Whittle Books, a business unit of Whittle Communications L.P. Books appear several times a year, and the series reflects a broad spectrum of responsible opinions. In each book the opinions expressed are those of the author, not the publisher or the advertiser.

I welcome your comments on this ambitious endeavor.

William S. Rukeyser
Editor in Chief

For Gene, John, and Ned

CONTENTS

INTRODUCTION

When interest rates started to tumble in 1991 and home-owners began their rush to refinance mortgages, J. Albert Smith Jr. knew he had a problem. Smith is the CEO of Banc One Mortgage, a major residential lender based in Indianapolis. His employees were already straining to keep pace with the firm's rapid growth, and now business was about to explode. That's a welcome problem, but a problem nonetheless. With tens of thousands of unemployed bankers across the country, the obvious solution was to hire a small army to handle the coming flood of mortgage applications. But instead of doing the obvious, Smith decided to reengineer Banc One's mortgage-application process.

Reengineering is the latest and most radical in an assortment of techniques that path-breaking chief executives have been using to achieve dazzling increases in productivity and competitiveness by rearranging the way work gets done. Taken together, these new ways of organizing work and workers constitute a productivity revolution that promises to transform American business—if only more CEOs will follow the lead of trailblazers like Al Smith. Later you will hear the details of what Smith did. For now, consider the results. In the first half of 1992, Banc One Mortgage's business shot up 153 percent with little increase in head count, and yet the average time to process an application dropped by almost a third. That's productivity.

America obviously has a productivity problem. Indeed, the entire world does. Productivity growth slowed significantly after 1973, and no industrial nation has yet returned to the heady progress that everyone enjoyed for nearly three decades following World War II. Economists have many theories but no solid explanation for the slowdown. The oil crises of the 1970s surely contributed. When oil prices multiplied, a substantial portion of the world's capital equipment, designed for an era of cheap energy, suddenly became inefficient and had to be replaced or rebuilt. The U.S. government may be to blame as well. Some studies indicate that a quarter of the drop-off in U.S. productivity growth reflects the costs of environmental and job-safety regulations.

The entry of baby-boomers and more women into the work force also played a role. The burgeoning supply of labor drove down its price, and wages of young, inexperienced workers failed to keep pace with inflation during much of the last 20 years. The inflation-adjusted wages of older workers continued to rise, but more slowly than at any previous time in the postwar era. All those comparatively cheap workers encouraged business to use relatively more labor and less capital. And productivity, of course, is directly related to the amount of capital equipment per worker.

Total capital investment did not decline. Investment as a percentage of gross domestic product has changed little over the postwar decades. But because the labor force was growing so fast, the rate of increase in the amount of capital per worker tumbled. From 1959 to 1973, capital per worker in the private sector grew 2.4 percent a year and productivity 2.8 percent a year. In contrast, capital per worker rose only 0.8 percent a year from 1973 to 1989, and productivity growth dropped to a rate of only 0.9 percent. (One bit of good news is that the labor force is growing much more slowly now, so the rate of increase in capital per worker should climb back up.)

Changes in demographics and regulatory policies in the U.S. cannot, however, explain the worldwide decline in productivity growth. In addition to the impact of costlier oil, one global productivity theory that makes sense revolves around the march of history. The postwar boom and its accompanying spurt in productivity were unprecedented, and some economists believe this wonderful era may have been a direct result of the Great Depression and the war. Just as rebuilding after the war drove growth in Europe and Japan and pent-up consumer demand spurred activity in the U.S., pent-up ideas and innovations on hold for more than a decade may have fueled productivity growth everywhere. If that theory is correct, at least part of the slowdown after 1973 was simply a return to more normal rates of progress.

Whatever its causes, poor productivity performance merits serious concern. Consider a single statistic: if U.S. productivity growth had stayed at its pre-1973 pace over the last 20 years, national income would be almost 40 percent higher today. In thinking about productivity, however, it is important to understand the true dimensions of the issue. That means putting aside some widely held misconceptions. One is that the U.S. is losing out in competitiveness. The rest of the industrial world did gain considerable ground on the U.S. from 1946 until around 1980. That was inevitable as Germany, Japan, and other nations built new industrial bases—and as they adopted U.S. know-how. But the relative performance suddenly reversed in the 1980s. Over that decade, U.S. productivity in manufacturing shot up at a 3.9 percent annual rate, faster than Germany's and even faster than Japan's. The much maligned U.S. worker is still 30 percent more productive than his Japanese counterpart, and U.S. per capita gross domestic product is 28 percent higher than Japan's.

The improvement in U.S. competitiveness has been obscured by enormous trade deficits, by the triumph of the Japanese in consumer electronics and automobiles, and by the protectionist pleadings of so many U.S. industries. The low growth in real wages since the early 1970s also contributes to the perception that we must be doing something very wrong. We are. Despite the stellar productivity performance by manufacturers, total productivity growth has not recovered. That is because productivity in service industries stopped growing or possibly even declined in the 1980s. Significantly, service companies have been much slower than manufacturers to adopt the techniques that will be described in this book.

So how do we get productivity back on track? In recent years, more than a score of study commissions have produced recommendations. Most suggest spending more on research and development, forging new bonds between industry and academe, and turning out more scientists and engineers. Those suggestions may have merit, but they are of the macro variety and provide scant guidance for a CEO or his company. In contrast, the techniques that CEOs like Al

Smith are using successfully are distinctly micro: they apply at the level of the company, division, or plant.

This volume is about those techniques and how chief executives can use them to lead their companies to higher levels of productivity, profits, and growth. The ideas presented here will sound familiar. No single term describes them all, so I will call them high-performance techniques, a term you may have heard used differently elsewhere. Here it encompasses methods such as employee involvement, work teams, and cell manufacturing. Most, apart from reengineering, have been around for 20 years or more. Every executive has heard about them, and most probably believe they understand them. However, if your company isn't using these techniques already (and few are), it means you don't really appreciate how powerful they can be. Only 10 percent or so of American companies have adopted high-performance techniques in a comprehensive way, and most have done so under duress. With few exceptions, CEOs have tried these measures only as a last resort to save their company from "going chapter" or their flagging subsidiary from being sold.

Thanks to the field-testing these pioneers have done, the other 90 percent of American companies (and companies elsewhere) now have a set of tools that can quickly produce quantum leaps in productivity—gains of 50 percent or more—in any company in any industry. No matter how good you think you are, these tools can make you better. What's more, the gains are virtually free. Adopting high-performance techniques usually involves some immodest consulting fees and training costs, but it does not require huge investments in new machinery or technology. In that sense, the higher profits these productivity gains produce really are found money.

This is not a comprehensive manual on how to implement high-performance techniques. Instead, my goal is to give you a better understanding of what these techniques are—and the power they possess—through examples of chief executives who have put themselves at the forefront of the productivity revolution. The experiences of the companies that have used high-performance techniques provide important lessons for every CEO. The companies reach across the spectrum, from mining and heavy manufacturing to high-tech and financial services. They have found keys to more efficient ways of doing almost anything, from managing accounts payable and processing mortgage applications to making bowling balls and assembling missile guidance systems.

One observation comes up again and again in conversations with chief executives who have ventured into this new world. Making these changes is hard work. Although they aren't expensive, high-performance techniques entail wrenching changes in the way companies are organized and managed, which is probably the biggest reason most companies have adopted them only as a last resort. In essence you are asking managers and workers to embrace new ways of operating, and altering long-established behavior is never easy. High-performance techniques bring a substantial reshuffling of power within an organization, something that most managers instinctively resist, especially when their jobs are at risk. As a result, success depends on enthusiastic leadership from the very top. Managing a revolution is not an assignment you can delegate.

What more timely subject for any CEO these days than productivity?

It is especially important to Cessna because Citation business jets are used by our customers to increase the productivity of their key employees.

There is simply no form of transportation that is even close in terms of flexibility, comfort and economy.

A Citation is viewed by an increasing number of companies as an essential ingredient in efficiently operating a business and improving productivity.

We are grateful for this opportunity to help our Citation owners become more competitive.

And having achieved almost 60 percent of the world's light and mid-size business jet market for three consecutive years, we are proud of our leadership in such an important industry.

As you evaluate productivity improvements for your company, I hope you'll include the capability we offer on your list.

Sincerely yours,

Russell W. Meyer, Jr.
Chairman and Chief Executive Officer
Cessna Aircraft Company

Cessna Aircraft Company · One Cessna Boulevard · Wichita, Kansas 67215 · 316/941-7400

Cessna
A Textron Company

Chapter One

THE PRODUCTIVITY REVOLUTION

Miners at Magma Copper like to tell the story of the morning in October 1989 when they arrived at work and were stunned to find chief executive J. Burgess Winter standing side by side with Harry R. Clark, president of the Boilermakers local, passing out leaflets at the gate. The scene marked the beginning of the remaking of the Arizona mining company. Winter and Clark had just returned from a two-day meeting in Scottsdale during which company executives and union leaders had agreed to work together to improve productivity and preserve jobs. The leaflets laid out the principles of "fairness, honesty, and integrity" that would govern a new Joint Union-Management Cooperation Committee.

The miners were properly cynical. Relations between Magma and its workers had always been awful and never more so than in the months since July, when they had signed a new contract. Productivity, never good, was in decline after the acrimonious settlement. The company had made several botched attempts at morale-building and employee involvement over the years, and by now the miners didn't believe anything the bosses said. Even so, they were impressed to see the chief executive, who had been with the company just over a year, greeting workers at the gate. Magma brass didn't do things like that. And there was Harry Clark standing right next to him, smiling.

Productivity at Magma Copper has risen 50 percent since 1989, when CEO J. Burgess Winter (left) and union president Harry R. Clark handed workers notice of a new era in union-company cooperation.

◆

Today almost everyone at Magma is smiling. In less than three years, productivity rose more than 50 percent companywide and more than 60 percent in the company's main mine in San Manuel, Arizona. The workers' jobs are secure, they got an unexpected $1.50-an-hour raise in 1991, and many are collecting bonuses equal to 10 percent of their wages. Some of the rank and file, so recently bitter and disenchanted, are as enthusiastic as plebes at an Army-Navy game. "I'm proud to work for Magma," says steelworker Fred Velasquez, "and I never said that for the first 13 years I worked here. For 13 years I got paid for something I had to do. For three years

I've been paid for doing things I enjoy." The transformation is equally visible in Magma's financials. The company is profitable and getting more so every quarter, and its stock price tripled in the first half of 1992.

The tale of how Burgess Winter transformed Magma Copper provides a vivid illustration of the powerful effect that attitudes alone can have on productivity. It also shows that for changes in attitude to take place, the chief executive's leadership is essential. The productivity improvements at Magma aren't the result of a huge investment in new equipment or a technological breakthrough. Some of the gains come from working smarter than before, but they mostly reflect what happens when disaffected employees start cooperating with management and with each other—when they simply try to do their jobs well. The methods Winter used to reshape Magma serve as a primer for any CEO who wants to take his company into the new age of participative management.

Participative management is a term that has many meanings. I use it to encompass a number of familiar buzzwords and phrases, including *employee involvement*, *self-managed work teams*, and (ugh) *empowerment*. It is the human side of a productivity revolution that started in the 1960s but didn't catch on until the mid-1980s. The techniques that compose participative management all have a decidedly touchy-feely sound to them. They are also highly derivative of Japanese management techniques, which may partially explain why so few companies have adopted them. Everyone has heard that work teams are powerfully productive, for example, but how many believe it?

These techniques work better than most people realize. Enough companies have experimented with participative management to prove that it can increase productivity in any company—provided the CEO is the one engineering the change. The transformation of Magma, for example, would not have been possible without the determined leadership of Winter, a towering, heavyset Irishman who has spent his working life managing mines in South Africa and the U.S. Winter is not a touchy-feely kind of guy. But he is "mildly anti-establishment," as he puts it, and he had deplored the mining industry's "Dark Ages" labor relations since he arrived in the U.S. in 1976. Winter had wanted to make similar changes at BP America's Kennecott Copper division when he was senior vice-president in charge of operations there from 1983 to 1988 but concluded that he had too little power to make the reforms stick. "You can't do anything about it," he says, "unless you're the head honcho."

Less than a year after moving to Magma, Winter knew he had to act. After signing its new labor contract in July 1989, the company needed a 20 percent increase in productivity to survive, an implausibility under the old regime. "It was pretty obvious we weren't going to get any productivity out of these guys," Winter says. So he turned to Marsh H. Campbell, Magma's vice-president for human resources and a seasoned labor-relations executive. Campbell, whose inclinations meshed with Winter's, called in consultant Robert P. Mueller to act as a sort of marriage counselor between management and the unions.

Mueller, who joined Magma as a vice-president three years later, first taught the bosses and workers how to talk to each other and to recognize their mutual interests—in short, to move from confrontation to cooperation. Winter, meanwhile, made sure his managers listened to Mueller. "When you're the boss, you can force changes," he says. "But [change] won't work if you don't drive it." At Magma, driving it meant that Winter had to replace or reassign every member of his senior management team, with the sole exception of Campbell.

With crucial cooperation from the regional and national offices of the United Steelworkers, which represents most of the company's workers, Magma quickly turned a horrendous labor situation into one of the best in the country—certainly the best in unionized hard-rock mining. Once the company and its unions had kissed and made up, Magma began reorganizing miners into work teams that are essentially self-managing. Supervisors, who had been cast in the mold of Simon Legree, have become "facilitators" who help workers solve problems instead of telling them what to do. The result is the 60 percent leap in productivity at San Manuel, and Magma says that is just an appetizer. An experimental "high-performance" team has achieved productivity increases of more than 100 percent, and Magma is gradually transferring many of the team's innovations to the entire mining operation. The company expects to enjoy additional outsize productivity gains each year through the mid-1990s.

The best news about the techniques that Burgess Winter exploited so successfully at Magma—which are explored in more depth in the next chapter—is that they can supercharge productivity at any company, no matter what its business and no matter how efficiently it is operating now. Says Jon H. Simpson, the former chief executive of Titeflex, an industrial-hose company in Springfield, Massachusetts: "I've personally been involved with 15 companies that did this, and they all got absolutely fantastic results." Yet as I have indicated, only 10 percent or so of American corporations have adopted any of these techniques, and most of those are companies like Magma that had to do *something* simply to remain viable. Even Motorola, the electronics company based in Shaumberg, Illinois, that has incorporated more of these techniques more successfully (and more enthusiastically) than any other giant corporation, acted only because the Japanese were killing it in the semiconductor and cellular telephone businesses.

The slow spread of these techniques isn't surprising given the natural skepticism about any radical idea—especially suggestions like turning quality control over to production workers and letting teams of blue-collar or clerical workers police themselves. The superiority of participative management has become the conventional wisdom in leading business schools, but it wasn't long ago that most professors dismissed it as psychobabble. What's more, any organization resists fundamental change, and these ideas almost always require a wrenching redistribution of authority (i.e., power) within a corporation. That is precisely why the chief executive has to be intimately involved. This isn't an assignment the boss can hand off to the head of manufacturing or operations.

Participative management and the other techniques that compose the productivity revolution are bound to spread much more rapidly over the next 10 to 20 years, which is cause for optimism about productivity in the U.S. For one thing, the conventional wisdom in business schools eventually becomes boardroom wisdom. For another, a legion of fee-hungry consultants is out there proselytizing this new religion. Says Harvard professor Richard E. Walton, a trailblazer in participative-management techniques: "Twenty years ago I and one or two others were the only ones who knew how to reorganize shop floors. Today thousands of consultants are equipped to help."

Most important, these techniques are so powerful that even today's most successful corporations—service companies as well as manufacturers—will ultimately be compelled to adopt them, as former Motorola chairman Robert W. Galvin was, simply to remain competitive. As that happens, national productivity should shoot up, conceivably matching the growth rates of the golden age of the

1950s and '60s. Meanwhile, the companies whose CEOs act first will gain a sharp edge on their competitors.

Surprising as it may seem in this age of buzzwords, no catchall term encompasses the assortment of innovations that make up the productivity revolution. These high-performance techniques go under many names, although they often describe actions so similar that only a mother could tell them apart. It seems as though every consulting firm has coined a special term to describe its subtle variation on a common theme. The following is a short list of the basics, all of which I'll explain later through examples of companies that have used them:

Participative management. This technique takes many forms, but the basic idea is that increasing worker involvement brings progressively better quality and lower costs. By giving shop-floor and clerical workers more latitude, responsibility, and information about the company's goals, they become more committed to the enterprise. "Empowered" workers are usually organized into teams of five to 25 people responsible for functions much more complex than those of any one individual (e.g., processing all aspects of an insurance application). Work teams are typically self-managing: they make the decisions about who performs which tasks on a given day, set goals, schedule production, overtime, and vacations, and are responsible for the behavior of team members. Says Michael Neuroth, a consultant who became a convert to participative management while working at Xerox and Combustion Engineering: "Empowerment means workers are truly empowered—not to buy pencils or other trivia, but to make the best product as they see fit."

Multiskilling. This practice encourages or requires workers to learn more than one job. It makes employees more flexible, enriches their jobs by adding variety and new challenges, and gives them a better appreciation of how their jobs fit into the whole. Equally important, it makes workers better at spotting defects. Typically, multiskilled workers learn many or all of the individual jobs assigned to their work team. Motorola turned to multiskilling when it made production workers responsible for quality control in its cellular telephone business. Lechmere Inc., a privately owned retail chain, used multiskilling at a store in Sarasota, where it encountered a shortage of entry-level workers. The Sarasota workers proved so much more productive than the Lechmere norm that the company, based in

Woburn, Massachusetts, exported the practice to other stores. Multi-skilled workers usually get raises for learning new jobs, a practice known as pay-for-knowledge.

Gainsharing. This is incentive compensation for the rank and file. As the name implies, it is a way of sharing the pecuniary rewards from increased productivity. Gainsharing most often takes the form of old-fashioned profit-sharing, although purists argue that profit-sharing doesn't create effective incentives and therefore doesn't qualify. Gainsharing works best when incentive payments are based on variables that workers can affect directly, such as production goals within a plant or office. In addition to being an incentive, gainsharing helps answer the frequent complaint that workers see little or no connection between their efforts and subsequent pay raises. Compensation consultants love it because it is difficult to do right.

Just-in-time manufacturing. This Japanese import should not be confused with just-in-time inventory controls, which almost every company says it uses today. JIT is at the heart of factory and office redesign. Sometimes called flow manufacturing, it is the application of just-in-time inventory-control principles to the production and distribution processes and often involves radical changes in production techniques and factory layout. JIT attacks work-in-process inventories by eliminating white space (the holding areas where partially completed goods sometimes wait weeks before moving to the next step on an assembly line). It also eliminates delays in order processing, setup and changeover times on machines, and the like. The basic goal is to reduce turnaround times and eliminate waste. The Boston Consulting Group has repackaged JIT manufacturing under the name time-based competition. Andersen Consulting of Chicago calls its variation time-compression management, or TCM. Says Leroy "Pete" Peterson, Andersen's managing partner of manufacturing: "If I can make and deliver a product in one-third the time of my competitor, I think I'll make three times as much money and grow three times as fast." JIT often uses manufacturing cells in place of assembly lines. A cell is a group of workers who make a complete product or subassembly in a small space or on a U-shaped line where each worker can perform one task and then turn around and do another.

Reengineering. This is the newest, most radical, and most potent change in organizational design. Consultant Michael Hammer, a leading purveyor of the technique and the person who coined the term, describes it as the radical redesign of business processes to eliminate procedures that do not add value to the final product, with emphasis on the words *radical* and *process*. At the heart of reengineering, says Hammer, is the notion of breaking away from outdated rules and fundamental assumptions that underlie operations. Instead of focusing on individual procedures, reengineers look at a complete process. And rather than streamline all the procedures in, say, processing an insurance application, reengineers first eliminate the nonessential tasks and then look for ways to accomplish the remaining ones more efficiently. As they do so, they wind up redefining functions and even entire processes.

Reengineering can produce mind-bending improvements. Ford reduced the number of employees in its accounts payable department by 75 percent. That's a 300 percent increase in labor productivity. ITT Sheraton used Hammer's model to reengineer its hotels and discovered that it could provide better service to guests while cutting the number of employees by 35 percent. More than any other technique, reengineering has to have leadership from the top. That is because it crosses departmental lines and cannot succeed without cooperation from the lords of different fiefdoms, each of whom wants to maximize the size and importance of his own empire.

Taken as a whole, these techniques constitute a revolutionary rethinking of how companies should manage employees and organize work, which is probably the major reason that few CEOs have embraced them. Many people seem to believe that high-performance techniques, most of which originated in Japan, cannot work in the U.S. because our culture is so different. U.S. workers don't sing company songs or do calisthenics on the shop floor, and no American company would dream of ordering office or factory employees to wear uniforms. However, those cultural differences obscure recent insights about how organizations operate most efficiently.

To see why these techniques work, it helps to understand that most conventional thinking about productivity has changed very little in the last century. The basic formula builds productivity by standardizing products, equipping assembly lines and offices with state-of-the-art machinery, keeping production runs long to capture economies of scale, and making tasks as simple and mindless as possible (that is, making them difficult to screw up). By this thinking, industrial engineers are best qualified to decide how jobs

IMAGINE A CITATION
THAT'S BEEN FLYING NONSTOP
SINCE THE YEAR 1307.

That's how much flight time Citation business jets have logged.
The fleet has accumulated an incredible six million hours of service.

It's the equivalent of one Citation flying night and day for 685 years.

It took more than just one to chalk up six million hours, of course.
Nearly 2,000 Citations are now in service – the world's largest fleet.

So if you're looking for the business jet that more businesses fly, just
look up. Chances are, there's a Citation passing overhead right now.

THE SENSIBLE CITATIONS

Cessna
A Textron Company

should be done. Supervisors then tell workers what to do and how to do it and, like cops on the beat, monitor them closely to make sure they perform as instructed. Add a union to the scene, and supervisors often take on the added responsibility of preventing alienated workers from actually damaging the company.

Under this system, "management" means control. Most management functions, and even entire departments, exist to control workers and materials—to ensure that the company performs as executives have decided it should. This fixation on control dates back to the work of Frederick W. Taylor, sometimes called the father of scientific management. Taylor conducted the first time-and-motion studies in 1881 when he watched laborers shoveling sand and devised ways they could do it faster. Most managers have been watching workers shovel sand ever since, defining jobs by lowest-common-denominator assumptions about employees' skills and motivation.

To make the control strategy work, managers divide tasks into rigid hierarchies of specialized roles reinforced by a top-down allocation of authority, salary, and status symbols. Twentieth-century science added enormous complexity to the technology of producing goods and services, along with elaborate mathematical models for measuring productivity, but the basic form of organizing work and workers has remained essentially unchanged. Most corporations and industrial engineers still try to reduce tasks to the simplest level even though new office and factory machines demand greater and greater skills.

Critics of the conventional approach say it leaves companies far short of the efficiency they could achieve with existing equipment and technology. For one thing, most corporations aren't measuring productivity properly, fancy tracking systems notwithstanding. W. Bruce Chew, a Harvard Business School professor and student of productivity in the U.S., Japan, and Europe, observes that the inappropriate productivity measures used by most companies lead to changes that do little to improve productivity or actually reduce it. The measurement systems are usually the creation of experts in cost accounting, statistics, and economics—people who design wonderfully sophisticated mathematical models but who often have little grasp of the challenges managers face. As Chew puts it, "Productivity measurement is simply too important to be delegated to productivity specialists."

The biggest flaw in most productivity measures—and most corporate efforts to improve productivity—is an overemphasis on direct labor costs. Chew cites the case of a company that spent $2 million a year to improve productivity. The company devoted 40 percent of its budget to reducing direct labor even though direct labor accounted for only 10 percent of manufacturing costs. Instead of focusing so narrowly on labor, productivity measures have to take account of how effectively a company uses all its resources, including materials, equipment, and, most important, support personnel. The basic question is, How good is your company at using all those "inputs" to produce goods or services? Focus too closely on one input, and a company will miss opportunities to improve the efficiency of others. High-performance techniques, in contrast, encourage everyone in the firm to focus on overall efficiency.

The overemphasis on direct labor is closely related to outdated cost-accounting systems. Measuring the material and labor content in any product is fairly simple, and when those systems were created at the beginning of the century, materials and direct labor made up the bulk of costs. Today, however, direct labor averages less than 15 percent of manufacturing costs and is often as low as 5 percent. The biggest cost component is now indirect overhead, which includes everything from depreciation to production planning, order processing, accounting and control, research and development, and a raft of other expenses.

Most accounting systems allocate this overhead according to the proportion of a company's total direct labor costs that goes into a given product. That has always produced distortions, because products that take the same amount of direct labor may require differing amounts of support and capital equipment. As direct labor has become a smaller portion of total costs, the distortion has multiplied. Among other things, this leads companies to price some products too high and others too low. When those distortions are layered onto productivity indexes, the result is an equally confused picture of overall efficiency.

Another problem with emphasizing a single factor (whether labor, output per machine, or output per unit of raw materials) is the ease of increasing the apparent productivity of any one factor by adding more of another. Labor, capital, and raw materials are all potential substitutes for one another. By substituting more machines or more materials for people, a company can achieve dazzling labor productivity even though it may have higher total costs. In contrast, many of the improvements that high-performance techniques generate come from reducing indirect costs. "We won't save much in direct labor costs—maybe 10 percent to 20 percent," says Pete Peterson of Andersen Consulting, who has probably been involved in the redesign of as many factories as anyone in the U.S. "But we get 30 percent to 50 percent reductions in indirect labor."

Fortunately, researchers have gained important insights in recent years into the variables that influence productivity and productivity growth. One of those researchers is Robert H. Hayes, another Harvard professor, who tracked productivity at 12 factories run by three corporations over a 10-year period. Like Chew, Hayes concludes that most managers are paying too much attention to direct labor and too little to other costs.

The most important discoveries in the Hayes study are how strongly waste, work-in-process inventories, and confusion affect productivity. Hayes expected to find a negative correlation between the percentage of materials wasted (or the percentage of rejects in production) and productivity, but he was amazed by its magnitude. It's not clear why waste is such a good indicator of poor productivity, but it is probably because waste normally results from other bad practices, including sloppy work.

Similarly, the increase in "total factor productivity," or overall efficiency, that came from cutting work-in-process (WIP) inventories was much greater than just the savings in working capital. Every reduction in WIP that Hayes examined was associated with an increase in total factor productivity. In one case, cutting WIP by 10 percent produced a 9 percent increase in total factor productivity. Hayes says this happens because the steps companies take to cut WIP usually lead to faster and more reliable delivery times and lower reject rates. But he cautions that cutting WIP alone will not produce great improvements. Instead, companies have to deal with the reasons for large inventories, which include long production changeover and setup times, volatile production schedules, and unreliable suppliers. The outsize gains associated with cutting WIP undoubtedly reflect the benefits of dealing with those problems. If a company doesn't deal with them, it needs its WIP as a safety net.

Managers torpedo productivity by erratically varying production rates, changing production schedules at the last minute, changing crews assigned to machines, and, perhaps most important of all, altering product specifications. The managers of the factories in Hayes's study blamed most of the resulting confusion on changes necessary to meet customer demands or to take advantage of new technology. Hayes demurs, saying that responding to new demands and seizing new opportunities does require change, but not confusion.

Ironically, minor changes are often more disruptive than major ones. Plant managers usually have warning of major changes and alert supervisors and train workers beforehand. Smaller changes, however, often get dumped on the shop floor with no preparation. Hayes suggests pressuring the engineers and the marketing department to put through only the most important changes and to design things right the first time. Finally, Hayes emphasizes continuous learning. When workers keep learning, plants get better and better. When workers don't learn, even the best plants go nowhere.

High-performance techniques attack each of the factors just cited. As often as not, however, the people who developed them had other objectives in mind. "The people doing the most exciting things are getting enormous productivity gains, but they don't see themselves pursuing productivity per se," says Seymour Tillis, a founding member of the Boston Consulting Group. "Instead, their emphasis is on quality, on turnaround times, or on working a social revolution in the workplace."

A central assumption behind the new factory and office designs, for example, is that the most important facet of competition is delivering services and defect-free products faster than anyone else. That's hardly news. All companies have had to learn that lesson, whether their products are microcomputers, life insurance policies, or bowling balls. As it turns out, intelligent approaches to quality improvement almost always reduce costs even though they often look expensive at the outset.

Quick turnaround times mean short production runs, anathema to managers schooled in economies of scale. But short runs don't have to mean higher costs. Since price matters as much as ever, the people looking for ways to accelerate design and production also had to make speed and quality cost-effective. In the process they have found simpler ways to get many jobs done, and simpler is cheaper. They also discovered they could eliminate many clerical and support functions that are supposedly crucial to the smooth running of organizations but more often just add delays and complexity. The rule of thumb is that any activity that does not add value for the customer is probably unnecessary.

The firebrands fomenting the social revolution that Sy Tillis refers to also assume that employees work much more effectively if you treat them with respect and give them more autonomy over what they do and how they do it. In the parlance of productivity expert Dick Walton, companies should abandon the strategy of imposing control over workers in favor of eliciting their commitment to the enterprise.

Sounds great, but can you really get commitment from high-school dropouts on an assembly line or clerical workers who barely made it through the Acme Home Study School of Word Processing? Absolutely. Powerful truths lie behind the hoary maxims that companies should employ a worker's mind as well as his hands and that the person doing a job understands it best. The experiences of Magma, Motorola, Banc One, and many others prove that beyond doubt.

Ford, for example, credits a large share of the efficiency gains it enjoyed when it began making the Taurus in the mid-1980s to participative techniques like asking assembly workers for ideas at the design stage. One suggestion was to put the same size head on all the bolts so that assemblers weren't constantly changing wrenches. That's an obvious idea but one that did not occur to the engineers—and that the workers did not contribute—until Ford began treating them differently. Motorola had unacceptably high failure rates in its cellular telephones in the mid-1980s. When the company shifted the responsibility for finding defects from quality inspectors to production workers, the defect rate fell 77 percent, from 1,000 per million parts in 1985 to 233 per million in 1989.

What Walton and his confreres are saying is that companies ought to regard rank-and-file workers the same way they regard managers. Managers (at least those who haven't burned out or been restructured out of a job) believe that their work will be judged individually, that superior performance will bring promotion, and that their bright ideas can win them equally bright rewards. A fresh-faced 19-year-old factory worker, on the other hand, quickly learns that it doesn't pay to offer suggestions. He may figure out a faster way to set up his lathe, but the foreman immediately makes it clear that he's there to do a job, not to change things. He sees few opportunities for advancement apart from those that come from seniority, and he also knows, especially if his is a union shop, that he won't be fired for anything other than stealing, doing drugs, or other egregious behavior. No wonder he's not committed.

Walton allows that the strategy of control probably made sense 40 or 50 years ago. Reducing tasks to the simplest level worked because the comparatively primitive equipment mechanized manual labor and required few skills to operate. When tasks are mindless, supervision supplies the sense of responsibility that line workers and clerks rarely bring to such jobs. In other words, it used to make sense to separate the physical (tasks) from the mental (supervision). Today's machines require significantly more attention and thought. That makes it much tougher for supervisors to monitor workers as closely or to impose responsibility as they once did. Rather than beat the wrong end of a dead horse, the workplace humanists argue, managers should put tasks back together so that workers can readily see the significance of what they are doing—that is, merge the physical and mental. Complicated jobs are more involving and satisfying, which helps foster commitment. And the new ensurer of responsibility among members of the work team is peer pressure.

Perhaps the biggest payoff comes from involving workers in finding solutions to problems. Proponents of continuous improvement policies (kissing cousins of total quality management) recognize that any process can be improved. The surest way of doing that is to engage workers in constant pursuit of the tiny improvements that eventually add up to world-class performance. How workers use machinery can be as important to productivity as the machines themselves. Consider NUMMI, the joint venture between GM and Toyota in Fremont, California. By most accounts, the NUMMI plant has been at least 50 percent more productive than any GM assembly plant, and its machinery is less up-to-date than most. Just as racing mechanics rely on the reactions and ideas of drivers, managers need constant input from workers to fine-tune today's equipment.

The productivity revolution has been building slowly for more than two decades, and it might not have happened at all without the impetus of tougher competition from abroad. "We owe a lot to the Japanese, because competition has forced managers to rethink," says Sy Tillis. "In the 1950s we felt we ruled the world. We won the war with very large companies, so productivity then meant scale. Almost 30 years later, by the mid-1970s, the old giants were getting the stuffing kicked out of them by foreign competition. It took 25 years longer than it should have to realize that something fundamental had changed. You need to walk into a wall before basic beliefs get rethought."

SENSIBLE BUSINESS DECISIONS GOT YOU WHERE YOU AR
THIS ONE TAKES YOU WHERE YOU WANT TO GO.

You've led your company through times in which others have failed. Thanks in no small part to your ability to act quickly and decisively.

But as the pace of the world quickens, you wonder if your company can continue to lead if it must follow airline schedules. For more than 1,500 businesses worldwide, the answer is no. They fly Citations.

It may surprise you to learn that a number of these companies are really not all that big. Yet.

<u>THE SENSIBLE CITATIONS</u>

Cessna
A Textron Company

Chapter Two

THE UNION TAMERS

t 2 o'clock on the morning of June 29, 1989—just four months before Magma Copper's CEO and the local union leader handed out those leaflets at the gate—a small charge of water-gel explosive ripped apart a security trailer on a hill overlooking the underground mine in San Manuel. An hour later and 40 miles to the south, a drive-by shooter fired a single bullet at the Tucson home of Magma CEO Burgess Winter.

Violence of that sort has been part of the landscape in hard-rock mining for more than a century, especially around contract time. Western mining companies have arguably had the worst labor relations in the U.S., and Magma fit the industry pattern. That June the company was locked in its most bitter negotiations ever with the United Steelworkers and six other unions, and a strike seemed likely. If the strike came, Magma was determined to break the unions, as Phelps Dodge had done at its Arizona mines five years before. Many of the workers were equally determined to bankrupt the company if it forced the unions out.

Magma and the unions hammered out an agreement three days after the bombing, but from the company's perspective the unions might as well have struck. The economic terms were livable, but relations between the bosses and the workers were not. "With negotiations like those, you don't just walk back into the mine the next day as if nothing had happened," says Donald H. Shelton, then president of the Steelworkers local. "This was a very delicate peace." Bitterness was visible on every face, and the miners seemed determined to lift as little ore as possible each day. Magma, which already had the highest-cost copper mine in the U.S. and a balance sheet enfeebled by a leveraged recapitalization a year before, was about to cave in.

In 1993, Magma is a company transformed. The ways Burgess Winter worked that transformation illuminate many of the problems in implementing participative management, especially if the workers belong to unions. Magma's success also shows why every chief executive with productivity problems ought to emulate Winter.

Union shops present special problems for participative management: it can't work without union cooperation. And unions have challenged its use in nonunion settings. In 1992, the National Labor Relations Board upheld a ruling against a then nonunion company for forming "action committees" of workers and managers. While the ruling may sound worrisome, most labor experts agree it was a narrow one not likely to prevail in future cases.

Still, union leaders have everything to lose and seemingly nothing to gain if workers start to love—or just trust—the company. Who needs unions in that kind of world? Furthermore, participative management and union work rules don't go well together. The object of participative management is to find faster, more efficient ways to get things done. Union work rules exist to create extra jobs and overtime. Even when the national union goes along, a company is likely to run into trouble from the locals. Ford Motor and the United Auto Workers found that out when they introduced participative-management practices on Ford's Taurus line, an initiative Ford called Team Taurus. Older workers hated watching "young kids" do jobs they had waited years to get. Officers of the locals felt compelled to complain, no matter what their leaders in Detroit were saying. The local unrest didn't derail the reforms, but it didn't help. Yet the experiences of Magma and other companies show that participative management can succeed in a union environment, provided the circumstances are right and top management is determined.

Magma's relations with its unions had reached a new low when the two sides met at the bargaining table in 1989. Three years before, the unions agreed to a 20 percent pay cut (from an average of

$15 an hour to $12) after watching the workers at Phelps Dodge and Cyprus vote out the unions. In return for the givebacks, Magma agreed to pay bonuses of up to $5.50 an hour if the price of copper climbed above $1.07 a pound. With copper selling then at 62 cents, no one believed the bonus provision would ever go into effect. Meanwhile, the givebacks accomplished nothing for Magma. "Costs kept going up because productivity went down," says Winter. "The workers were bitter and pissed off, so the givebacks didn't do the company a bit of good."

Then the price of copper shot up above $1. Good news, to be sure, but not good enough for Magma. In 1987 and '88 the company had to borrow $55 million from its banks to pay the bonuses, and in 1989, under a clause that tied them to the volume of production, Magma stopped paying the bonuses. The company blamed the low production on problems with its smelter, an excuse the unions didn't buy. Magma prevailed in grievances they filed with the NLRB.

With a recession looming and copper prices heading back south, Winter went to the bargaining table determined not to lose the $3-an-hour giveback. He was prepared to break the unions if they struck. The company put in a score of trailers to house replacement workers during a strike, brought in security police, and sent letters to workers inviting them to stay on the job (Arizona is a right-to-work state). Marsh Campbell, Magma's vice-president for human resources, says he believes the company's obvious resolve is what persuaded the unions to settle for a $1.50-an-hour raise.

A strike could have been devastating. Among other things, union members had sabotaged the trailers that replacement workers were to sleep in. "They had union people set up the trailers," says Don Shelton. "When the contract was signed, our guys raced back to disconnect the trailers so management wouldn't see what we had done. They put rags in the water drains. They screwed up the electricity. They ran the water lines to sewer water." Others apparently had more drastic things in mind. "The guys were talking about putting sand in the crankcase," says a miner. "The destruction would have been total." James F. Daley, then a supervisor in the San Manuel mine, was so alarmed by the tension that he considered sending his 15-year-old son out of town if a strike came.

In the acrid aftermath of the settlement, Winter began looking for ways to improve labor relations. He was fighting for the survival of the company. Magma, which Newmont Mining had spun off to shareholders in 1987, had the highest debt ratio in the mining industry. With copper prices almost certain to drop below $1 a pound, the company was doomed unless it could cut costs. That meant getting more productivity out of its workers, because labor makes up 60 percent of the costs in the San Manuel mine, the source of most of Magma's ore.

Marsh Campbell called Robert Guadiana, district director of the United Steelworkers for the region that includes Arizona, and convinced him that Winter wanted to make a fresh start with the unions. Guadiana then persuaded his superiors in Pittsburgh to let him work with the company. Campbell correctly surmised that officers of the locals would come to the table only if they were ordered to by the national. He had approached Don Shelton several times outside the contract negotiations and got nowhere. "I told him to get away from me before something happened that we both would regret," says Shelton. Campbell also recognized that because the unions' distrust of the company was total, they would have to get a third party to act as an honest broker.

The first and only third party the company and unions interviewed was Bob Mueller, a former Ford executive who had worked on Team Taurus and was then consulting with Manville on its relations with unions. Guadiana called John Kerrigan at the Steelworkers local (Shelton was on vacation) to tell him to go to Los Angeles with three other union officers and four company executives to interview Mueller. Kerrigan hung up on Guadiana twice and agreed to go only after Guadiana reminded him that the contract contained a clause about cooperation and warned that the national would take action against the local if he refused. Shelton, a volatile bear of a man, returned from vacation several weeks later and was furious when he learned Kerrigan had been on a junket with the bosses. He was madder still when he learned he had to attend the watershed meeting in Scottsdale. "I called Guadiana and shouted at him for 40 minutes, but I was bound by that cooperation clause," he says.

The two-day meeting at the McCormick Ranch in Scottsdale opened with a cocktail party the night before the first session. The scene was like a dancing class for 12-year-olds, with company executives bunched on one side of the room and union officers on the other. When Winter and Campbell invited the union officers to dinner, they refused. Mueller told the group it would be a successful meeting if there was no blood on the walls.

The next morning, Mueller had both sides vent their anger and accusations. Then, in classic mediator fashion, he helped them sort out facts from prejudices and opinions. Toward the end of the day the two sides were beginning to recognize that they had a common problem much larger than their problems with each other. Mueller had everyone break off in pairs—Shelton and Campbell, for example—and interview one another about their families, hobbies, and the like. It was airy-fairy stuff, Shelton says, but it helped. Both sides agreed to form the Joint Union-Management Cooperation Committee (JUMCC) on the second day, and Winter and Guadiana prepared the new committee's mission statement. "It worked because Winter was willing to put the mission statement in writing," says Shelton. "I don't believe anything unless it's in writing."

Now all they had to do was sell this package to the 1,500 miners in San Manuel and 600 others at Pinto Valley, an open-pit mine near Globe, Arizona. Nothing substantial could happen until the rank and file believed real change was in the works. Winter didn't have the luxury of gradually phasing in the new regime, so Magma proceeded on many fronts at once. In the first half of 1990 the company replicated the two-day Scottsdale session for groups of 30 to 50 union members, supervisors, and managers. The sessions took place at Biosphere II (then known as Sunspace), an enormous hermetically sealed glass dome about midway between Tucson and San Manuel. Some 700 employees attended the sessions.

Magma also put all its supervisors and union stewards through seven-day courses in participative-management and team-building techniques. "This was vital," says Winter. "Most of them had come up through the union and knew only the contractual way of doing business. Now we were asking them to become different kinds of supervisors—facilitators, coaches, and resource suppliers." The company included the stewards in the classes to prove to them that it wasn't lying about change and to allow them to form partnerships with individual supervisors. The continuing partnerships have helped smooth the transition to work teams. They also created some unlikely alliances. John Kerrigan, for example, says he gets on famously with his management partner now, but in 1989, "I wouldn't have walked across the street to piss down his throat if his stomach was on fire."

Still, many workers—and many supervisors—remained unconvinced. Some believed the company had somehow captured the unions

EARLY IN HIS CAREER, MR. PALMER TURNED IN HIS CONVENTIONAL DRIVER FOR SOMETHING WITH CONSIDERABLY MORE LOFT.

Years ago, Arnold Palmer quit using automobiles for traveling to golf tournaments. For almost as long as we have built Citation business jets, Arnold Palmer has flown them.

Without the speed, convenience and reliability of Citations, Arnie says he couldn't possibly compete on the tour, design more than 100 golf courses, and manage his far-ranging business activities.

Mr. Palmer's game is golf, but his business is winning. So is his business jet.

THE SENSIBLE CITATIONS

Cessna
A Textron Company

and that nothing fundamental was going to change. Others thought the whole thing was a bad idea. Says Daniel A. Valensuela, a coordinator at San Manuel: "Frontline supervisors were very leery of being cut back. When Sunspace started, I had just become a manager again. I had been demoted earlier for not being tough enough. Now we were being told we shouldn't be tough. I just didn't see how this could work." Campbell says he was surprised to find so little support among people who had been to Sunspace. "After the two-day meetings, people were charged up about the possibilities but discouraged by the paucity of real progress."

Progress came slowly in other areas, including action on specific grievances that the unions had raised in Scottsdale. Magma set up problem-solving teams, but solutions sometimes proved elusive. One complaint had to do with contracting out work at the mines to other companies. The craft unions in particular wanted to preserve this work for their members and asked Magma to abolish the practice. The company refused to surrender its flexibility, although Campbell says it has asked the unions to "bid" on some projects and has awarded a few to them. The two sides also failed to agree on Magma's request to start a drug-testing program. "There is a lot of booze and drugs in mining towns, so it is politically delicate for union leaders," says Campbell. "It puts them in the position of enforcing prohibition."

Magma had better luck on less political issues. The most important of all involves the Kalamazoo ore body at the San Manuel mine. Since mining began in 1956, San Manuel has yielded nearly 600 million tons of ore-bearing rock, more than any other underground hard-rock mine in the world. The main ore body, called the San Manuel, will be mined out by 1997. The adjacent Kalamazoo, or the K, as Magma calls it, may contain more ore than the San Manuel, but it is deeper and more expensive to mine. By 1989 Magma had invested more than $150 million in preliminary development of the K and concluded that it could not get the ore out profitably at current costs—which meant that everyone in San Manuel would be out of a job after 1997.

The biggest carrot that Winter held out to the unions was the possibility that higher productivity could make the K viable and extend the life of the mine to 2008 or beyond. In February 1990 he formed a management-union design team to prepare a plan for the K. The following October a "high-performance" team of 150 volunteers began mining the K at 2,900 feet below ground level. The team could ignore union work rules and had much greater control over operating decisions, along with improved communications between work crews and greater job flexibility. When it began hauling ore that October, the cost was an unacceptably high $7 a ton. By December 1990 the cost was down to $5.25, and a year later it was $3.80— less than the cost (at the time) of lifting ore from the San Manuel ore body. By the end of 1992 it appeared almost certain that Magma would go ahead with full development of the K.

Attitudes gradually improved as union officers and workers saw real changes in 1990 and early 1991. Says Harry Clark, who has been president of the Boilermakers local for more than 25 years: "At the end of the Scottsdale meeting, I thought we would go back to the status quo and wondered if we were setting ourselves up for our own destruction. Then came the Sunspace sessions, when Winter said managers who couldn't adapt had to go." If the statement that managers and supervisors might be fired was impressive, actual firings were doubly so, although Magma discharged only 15 supervisors out of more than 500 in the first two years of the JUMCC.

Magma's managers, however, fared much worse than its supervisors. Winter replaced the senior executives in charge of the San Manuel mine and a group of managers at Pinto Valley. Like San Manuel, the Pinto Valley mine has two possible futures. Under one, the ore that can be mined profitably will be exhausted by 1999. But if Magma can get costs low enough, the mine could operate for at least an extra seven years. By 1991, costs were dropping fast in San Manuel, but not at Pinto Valley, where the managers were less receptive to the new spirit of cooperation. "They all fought the program at Pinto Valley," Winter says. "I lectured them. I counseled them. Finally, I terminated all of them in one day."

Among the departing were the Pinto Valley general manager, the mine manager, and the head of human resources. Winter turned Pinto Valley over to a young mining engineer named K. Lee Browne, who looks like he would be more at home on an Ivy League campus than at an open-pit mine in the Inspiration Mountains. But Browne has been getting the results Winter wants. He took over as interim manager in November 1991; by the first quarter of 1992, productivity at Pinto Valley was up 20 percent. By March 1992, mining costs dropped from a high of 59 cents a ton to 54 cents, and Browne's goal was 45 cents by the end of 1993. (As the figures suggest, open-pit mining is much cheaper than underground mining, but the underground ore is higher grade.)

Throughout this period, Magma and the unions were at work on a gainsharing plan that would give workers a clear self-interest in improving productivity. Most motivational experts agree that gainsharing can be a wonderful stimulant for workers. The obvious purpose is to tie compensation to the fortunes of the firm so that employees have an incentive to do their jobs better. The other attraction for managers is that gainsharing converts a portion of fixed costs to variable ones that arise only when the company does well. It also addresses a frequent complaint of workers, a majority of whom, according to surveys, see little connection between their efforts and subsequent pay raises.

The only difficulty with gainsharing—and it is enormous—is getting the formula right. Old-fashioned profit-sharing, most experts agree, doesn't do the job; too many factors that affect the bottom line are outside the control of workers. The workers know that, so profit-sharing usually has little impact on how they perform. True gainsharing, in contrast, ties bonus payments to goals workers understand and can strive to meet, such as unit costs in an individual plant. A variant on gainsharing, typically found in factories or offices that use multiskilling, is pay-for-knowledge. Motorola, for example, gives raises to workers in its cellular telephone plant when they learn a new skill. Helene Curtis does the same in its plastic-bottle factory, and the company has switched from multiskilling to a modest gainsharing plan in its main manufacturing plant.

Gainsharing and other variable-compensation schemes came into fashion in the 1980s. The American Productivity & Quality Center in Houston estimates that more than 75 percent of U.S. employers now use at least one form of nontraditional pay and says a large majority of those were adopted in the 1980s. However, the bulk of incentive-pay action has been timid. Most nontraditional pay plans, including the ones started in the 1980s, are profit-sharing. By the Productivity Center's calculations, fewer than 15 percent of U.S. companies have gainsharing plans. What's more, incentive plans rarely make up a significant portion of total pay. Japanese workers get an average of 25 percent of their total compensation in the form of a flexible bonus. In the U.S. the figure is 1 percent.

Magma's experience shows how much work goes into crafting an intelligent gainsharing program—and how much work can come out of it. Marsh Campbell began a serious investigation of gainsharing early in 1990. "The 1989 contract had a commitment to study gainsharing," he says. "Until then I had only read about it, but I saw that there could be a lot of power in a combination of gainsharing and employee involvement." So Campbell formed yet another team of executives and union officials to figure out what Magma should do. For the next six months, the team talked with consultants and made trips around the country to visit companies with gainsharing plans. "We learned a lot," Campbell says. "And the trips also were an opportunity to forge relations with the union reps. That's when we really began talking as human beings."

The gainsharing committee concluded that Magma needed a separate plan for each of its three operating divisions—the San Manuel mine, the Pinto Valley mine, and Magma Metals (the smelter, a copper-rod plant, and the marketing group). Each plan bases payments on three variables. The first, of course, is productivity. The second is materials usage, basically a reward for reducing waste, and the third is safety. Next, a committee for each business unit had to figure out the specific formulas. How much of a productivity increase should go to shareholders and how much to workers? Should the workers share any gains from productivity increases that resulted from purchases of new equipment?

Under the Magma system, gainsharing committees made up of management and union reps calculate an annual formula for each division based on historic performance and the year's goals. If a division exceeds its goals, workers get 40 percent of the savings as quarterly gainsharing payments. Since workers get bonuses only for exceeding, not just meeting, goals, union reps must have a role in determining the targets. Otherwise workers would complain that management was setting the bar higher than anyone could jump.

Magma unveiled its gainsharing programs with great fanfare in the second half of 1991. Both the company and the unions had reason to boast. The plans are the first in a U.S. copper mine. Although gainsharing has become commonplace in coal mines, especially nonunion ones, no other copper company had taken this step. More important, Magma's bonuses can equal 20 percent of wages in a standout year, which makes them far higher than most. From the union perspective, gainsharing represented the financial payoff from cooperation. The San Manuel miners made out handsomely under the plan in 1991. They collected payments averaging 13.6 percent of wages for the third quarter and 15.6 percent for the fourth. Pinto Valley and the smelter, on the other hand, failed to reach their goals, and workers got nothing. Says Winter: "In trying to sell this program, I was predicting that awards could be $3,000 to $5,000 a year. That's where they were in 1992."

Another big change at Magma is openness about company data, standard fare under participative management. Experts say workers become much more involved when managers tell them what the goals are in specific areas (such as operating rates, unit costs, defect rates, and waste levels) and give them regular updates on how a plant or division is doing. Fifteen years ago, editors at *Fortune* magazine marveled at charts in Japanese factories showing trends in productivity and celebrating the fact that it took fewer and fewer workers to turn out products. Today those same kinds of charts dot the walls of participatively managed factories in the U.S., and U.S. workers follow them with the same enthusiasm as their Japanese counterparts. These workers seem to understand that higher productivity isn't a threat to their jobs but a way to create more jobs by reducing costs and prices and thus boosting demand for a company's products.

At Magma, everyone has access to more information about the company's costs than middle managers at most companies ever see. Ask any miner at San Manuel, and he or she will quote the net cost per ton of ore mined last month and for the year to date. That kind of information-sharing is essential under a gainsharing plan because the incentive effect diminishes rapidly when workers can't see how they are doing. Winter didn't wait for gainsharing, however. He opened the company's books to the workers as soon as the JUMCC began. "Ours is a very secretive industry," he says. "Openness helped a lot in building trust. We showed the unions all our operating figures and our estimates of the comparable figures for the competition and laid out exactly what the problem was."

Once the matter of gainsharing was resolved, Winter put Campbell and the unions to work drafting a new contract. The contract then in effect didn't expire until July 1992, but Winter wanted a guarantee of long-term labor peace before he would consider spending up to $90 million more to develop the K. In the summer of 1991 a group of 80 management and union representatives broke into six problem-solving teams to draft the contract. Instead of the normal adversarial bargaining in which each side brings its proposals to the

IN 1995,
PEOPLE AROUND THE WORLD
WILL BEGIN DOING THE SIX-SECOND MILE.

You're looking at the fastest business jet in the world. At Mach .9, it does a mile in 6.06 seconds. And sprints LA-to-New York in under four hours.

It's the new Citation X. And it's the latest example of Cessna's commitment to the development of new technology. Our total investment in business aircraft research and support is now more than a billion dollars.

You can see for yourself the remarkable result of that investment when Citation X deliveries begin in 1995. But you'd better look fast.

THE SENSIBLE CITATIONS

Cessna
A Textron Company

table, the labor and management representatives drafted and took proposals to the table jointly. "The contract wasn't bartered or hammered out," says Winter. "It just emerged from problem-solving negotiations." The method was so radical that it required approval from the national offices of all the unions. Some of the craft unions protested, but the Steelworkers brought them into line. "To the extent that we have had resistance, the Steelworkers at the national level leaned on the other nationals," says Campbell.

By October 22, more than eight months before the old contract expired, Magma had a new one unlike any other in the U.S. It is a 15-year agreement, with economic terms specified for the first five years. If the company and the unions cannot agree on an economic package beyond that time, either side can opt for one-year binding arbitration and can do the same thing a year later. Thus, the contract guarantees that Magma will have no strikes or lockouts for seven years. The contract also formalizes the role of union-management work redesign teams modeled on the one in the K ore body. At the time it was approved, labor lawyers said the Magma contract was the first ever to include both an arbitration and a work-team clause. Finally, the contract restored the other $1.50 an hour the unions had surrendered in 1986.

It is difficult to get an exact fix on how the rank and file reacted to the new regime during the first two years. Some were enthusiastic from the start, and productivity began to improve almost immediately, at least in the San Manuel mine. But most workers still didn't trust management as late as April 1991, more than 18 months after the process began. That's when Don Shelton came up for reelection as president of the Steelworkers local and lost. His opponent was Manuel Medina, a former president of the local and a man who never got along with Shelton. Although his victory stemmed partly from ethnic politics (a majority of the members are Hispanic), Medina also used Shelton's cooperation with the JUMCC against him in the campaign. That's one more indication of the high stakes people face in making these changes and one more reason it's tough to adopt new methods: power structures change. A year later Medina was saying that he had become a strong supporter of the JUMCC and had raised questions about it only because Shelton kept him in the dark about what was happening even though he was an officer of the union.

By the middle of 1992, Magma had won the trust of all but about

20 percent of the workers. "We still have pockets of members who haven't climbed on," says Medina. "That's because their supervisors haven't changed, so their jobs haven't changed. They don't see anything different." Marsh Campbell says the craft unions are still resistant to changes in work rules and cites another interesting source of tension: "A self-directed work team creates a better schedule for itself. Then more senior workers with worse schedules or conditions complain. The unions don't want to say no to those guys, and some union officials are reluctant to say they coauthored the changes."

Union officials and supervisors say that gainsharing is what ultimately convinced most workers to support the program. The other big persuader was the final push to bring everyone into the program, which began a couple of months after the contract was signed. Over a 10-month period in 1992, Magma conducted two-day seminars on work redesign for every company member. Says supervisor Dan Valensuela: "The workshops do turn people around. Some go from being troublemakers to strong supporters of the program. They realize the company is spending money on this, so it must be serious."

The seminars were conducted by mine managers, supervisors, union stewards, and work-redesign facilitators hired by Bob Mueller. One facilitator is Charlie Lewis, a great-nephew of former United Mineworkers president John L. Lewis. Mueller had worked with Lewis at Manville, where he was president of a Glass Molders local for 12 years. Like Don Shelton, Lewis was voted out of office after he supported cooperation with management. During the seminars, senior managers laid out the goals for each division and explained that the workers are the ones who will figure out how to reach them. Then the instructors explained all the basics of teams and work redesign and the mechanisms Magma has in place for listening to ideas and implementing changes. "In the environment we have created, employee involvement is infectious and coercive," says Winter. "Everybody has ideas on how to do his job—or somebody else's job—much better. The opportunity to elucidate, design, and help to achieve improvements is insidious and irresistible, particularly when it results in hard-dollar rewards."

A few figures show just how enormous the rewards have been. The net cash cost per ton of ore mined in San Manuel dropped from $5.50 in 1989 to $4.20 in 1991. The goal for 1992 was $4 a ton; by year's end the cost was down to $3.99. The cost of smelting and refining copper has dropped 8 percent, from 17.7 cents a pound to

16.3 cents. The smelter finally achieved its promised efficiency (it has been running at 107 percent of rated capacity), and Magma has been operating the flash furnace without rebuilding it for more than four years, longer than any other company has achieved. The reject rate in the rod plant dropped from 18 percent in 1991 to 13 percent in 1992. "All that," says supervisor Kevin Carpenter, "was done by the workers."

When you press workers about how they achieved such improvements, the answer is always attitudes. They say the only things they are doing differently is cooperating with one another and paying attention on the job. Under the old regime, workers practiced what they call malicious obedience, meaning that they did exactly what a supervisor told them even when they knew the result would be harmful. One day in 1989, for example, a supervisor told a worker to go to a lower level in the San Manuel mine and make sure a water pump was operating. It was, but the pump burned out two hours later because the worker neglected to mention it was pumping dry.

Another change is cooperation among the supervisors leading different work crews. In the San Manuel mine, crews working on one level cut ore-bearing rock away from the mine wall (they call it pulling muck). Then they drop the muck through chutes and into rail cars run by crews working one level below. "In the old days," says supervisor Jim Daley, "crews that had to cooperate working at different levels would enter the mine from different places and never see each other above ground. A crew pulling muck complained about not having cars to haul it, and the crew running the cars complained about having no muck. Each supervisor would blame the performance of his crew on the other one. Now they discuss what they're doing on a shift before they go down and help each other out. Everyone is doing a better job because of it."

Workers have also come up with suggestions that save labor and materials. One involves the underground railroad tracks that carry ore cars. Each car contains 20 tons of muck, so the mine goes through track pretty fast. To replace the 33-foot steel rails, workers have to move them to an elevator cage, where they are suspended vertically and lifted to the top or lowered into the mine. The flanged rail wheels ride on the inside of the rail, so only that side of the rail wears down. After the new program began, a miner suggested simply shifting a worn rail to the other side of the track so that the unworn half is on the inside.

One of the most profound changes is in the relationships between supervisors and workers. In the past, they were enemies who didn't speak to each other off the job. The mining companies liked it that way because they believed supervisors needed to use harsh discipline to keep miners in line. Not long ago one mining company actually required workers to move to a different part of town when they were promoted to supervisors. Jim Daley and Sonny R. Edds, a mechanic, are friends now and display an uncommon camaraderie and sense of joint mission. Says Edds: "One of the things no one expected is that this has opened up new friendships that never were possible before."

Daley and Edds, both believers in the new system, talk a lot about "process" and "changing the paradigm." What they are saying is that the process of figuring out how to work together to solve problems has involved them in ways that never existed before. "For the first time, we are being treated like human beings," says Edds. "We don't just collect a paycheck from Magma. We are part of Magma." Adds Daley: "These guys aren't educated, but many of them are very smart. Now the company is listening to them. You can't imagine what a difference that is."

Magma could not have won its war without the cooperation of the locals and the United Steelworkers. The company got that cooperation, Winter says, because it had crucial leverage over the unions. Arizona lost more than 50 percent of its copper industry in the 1980s, and by 1989 Magma employed about two-thirds of the union miners in the state. Winter's lever was that San Manuel would close in 1997 and Pinto Valley in 1999 unless productivity increased significantly. If Magma did get the productivity gains it needed, he could guarantee another 26,000 man-years of union membership. "And membership is all that matters to unions," he says.

The Steelworkers had little choice but to go along with Magma. The alternatives probably were that Magma go broke or its employees vote the union out. In any event, the Steelworkers have put themselves at the mercy of the company by helping implement the new system. If a showdown came, a majority of the workers would side with the company. But a showdown is unlikely. The union now plays an important role in administering the new management system.

Jon Simpson had similar leverage over workers who belonged to the Teamsters when he became chief executive of Titeflex Corpo-

CEO Jon H. Simpson persuaded Titeflex employees to try teamwork and problem-solving techniques that ultimately saved the company. Simpson stands in front of a mural illustrating several company projects.

◆

ration in 1988. Titeflex, based in Springfield, Massachusetts, is a small (about $60 million a year) manufacturer of specialized Teflon and metal hoses for the aerospace, automotive, and industrial markets. Simpson, however, didn't need the national or even the local union leadership when he reshaped Titeflex. Instead, he worked with the chief steward in the Titeflex factory, who kept officers of the local in the dark until the changes were well along.

Titeflex was on a going-out-of-business trajectory when Simpson arrived. Although the company had a reputation for performing brilliantly on "impossible" jobs for NASA, its routine work was subpar. The company was consistently late with deliveries, its profit margins were unacceptably low, and it was losing market share year after year. The company had started in 1916 in Newark, New Jersey, and moved to Springfield in 1956 when it merged with the Indian Motorcycle Company. Bundy Corporation, a Detroit automotive parts manufacturer, acquired Titeflex in 1978, and then TI Group PLC, a British holding company, bought Bundy in 1988. TI immediately announced plans to sell Titeflex, sending the usual chills through the company, but instead hired Simpson to turn it around.

Simpson, then 41, had just converted CHR Industries, a New Haven maker of pressure-sensitive tape for the aerospace industry, to a participative-management system and set out to do the same at Titeflex. Simpson says he turned to participative management in the mid-1980s. "I started out in the Genghis Khan school of management," he says. "After a few years I realized it wasn't getting the company anywhere, so I decided to try something else. This was a very radical change for me."

Simpson brought aboard Michael Neuroth, formerly with Xerox and Combustion Engineering, as his head of operations. Neuroth says he first tried to "evolve" the changes at Titeflex but ran into massive resistance from managers, which didn't surprise him. "I have never seen this work under the old organization structure," he says. "It upsets the power structure, so those with power defeat it. Everyone is in favor of this for someone else." Next Neuroth appointed a small design team to rethink the entire operation. "I told them to start over, from scratch, and redesign this business," he says. "I made two guarantees to the team members: they all would have jobs when this was over, and no one would have the same job." Amazing as it may seem, the redesign took less than two weeks.

The basics of the new design were unremarkable. Titeflex reorganized itself into five business units, each of which makes a family of products (e.g., automotive hoses). But the transition to work teams and participative management was anything but ordinary. Simpson first enlisted the support of Ralph Galarneau, chief shop steward for the 300 Teamsters members in the plant. "I saw 'empowerment' as a way to break the union," says Galarneau. "But Jon asked us to help design and implement the changes. I knew we had to do something, so I agreed to go along. But I said there would be no concessions and that the whole thing was over with the first lie." Galarneau didn't tell his superiors at Local 404 about the changes. "I was worried about how the local would react, so it was about four months before I told the president what was going on."

Neuroth regrouped the manufacturing workers into teams and work cells, fired most of the shop foremen, and turned over the selection of team leader to a committee of five union representatives and only two from management. After the usual training in teamwork and problem-solving techniques, Titeflex made the change to work cells over a single weekend in the fall of 1989. Titeflex had had a conventional factory, with assembly lines that snaked through a rambling old building on the east side of Springfield. (The original owner was Rolls-Royce Ltd., which built the plant in the teens and assembled cars there for about 10 years.) Today the factory is divided into cells where teams of five to 15 workers fabricate complete hoses. The teams themselves designed their cells, placing machines where they could use them most effectively.

Simpson and Neuroth also reorganized some of the support functions, most notably order processing. Purchase orders used to go through six departments before they reached the shop floor, usually eight to 10 weeks after they arrived. Now all orders go through one "genesis" team that includes a contract administrator, an applications engineer, a design engineer, a draftsman, a production planner, and an order-entry clerk. It still takes about two weeks to process an order, because most require custom engineering, but Titeflex can produce price quotes in 24 hours. In the old days, Titeflex quoted 18 weeks delivery on orders but took an average of 30 weeks to fill them. "Rush" orders frequently sat for weeks between departments. Now the company quotes eight to 10 weeks delivery, and its on-time performance has been as high as 90 percent.

Titeflex got the startling improvements that have become so ordinary in participatively managed facilities. Scrap is down more than 90 percent in some product lines, work-in-process inventory dropped more than 70 percent, the number of returned orders is down from nearly 30 a month to seven—about half of those because of paperwork problems—and the number of union grievances dropped from about 25 a month to 14 in the first three years under the new system. Simpson says his goal was to "double and halve," meaning that he wanted to double profits while halving lead times and inventories. He set out to reduce overhead 40 percent in the first two years. He cut it in half, partly by slashing the number of salaried workers from 280 to 170 as the reorganization made their jobs unnecessary. (No production workers lost their jobs because of the changes.)

Simpson and Neuroth's methods also produced some changes that don't seem quite so common. Simpson began a practice of taking customers directly to the shop floor when they had complaints about Titeflex products. Galarneau says that had a much greater impact on workers than any amount of explaining or browbeating by supervisors. Neuroth insisted, over the strenuous objections of the marketing department, on sending shop-floor workers to meet with customers. "The marketing people were adamant that we couldn't send hourly workers to General Electric's jet engine plant," says Neuroth. "I sent them anyway—the next day. Before they got back here, GE called to thank us for sending floor workers. They were flattered. 'Any company can send the president,' a GE executive said, 'but sending factory workers showed how important we are to you.'"

The trip, and others like it, had an interesting effect on the workers. When they saw all the hoses made by competitors on GE engines, they realized how much business the Titeflex marketers were missing. Chris Ward, head of the hose-fabricating business unit, says it was suggestions from hourly workers that led the marketing department to go after time-sensitive orders. "We had no idea until this happened how much of a premium some customers will pay for faster delivery," he says.

Titeflex's sales per employee are up, expenses per sales dollar are down, and the company is much more profitable, although Simpson, now in charge of market planning at TI Group's offices in Washington, D.C., won't say how profitable. The company got through the recession with only three layoffs, and all three people were back in five weeks or less. Says Neuroth, who now owns a consulting business in Wilbraham, Massachusetts: "Unions are not a problem. It is management at union companies that is the problem."

The most important factors behind the successes at Magma and Titeflex clearly were Winter and Simpson. "Jon Simpson was committed," says Galarneau. "That was the most essential ingredient." At Magma, miners, union presidents, and managers all mention how Winter kept pushing the program forward and say that he made the difference. Looking back, Winter stresses how difficult it was to make the changes. "Other companies are looking for a $50,000 package they can buy off the shelf for a quick fix," he says. "But this is hard work. There's a period where it's very hard and you don't see any results. You just have to keep pushing and make certain that everyone goes along." Winter hopes that what Magma has done will become a model for union relations elsewhere. He has been encouraged by all the attention the company has received. Executives from Arco, Mobil, American Airlines, and a host of other companies, including ones in Chile and Argentina, have visited Magma to learn its lessons. Interestingly, though, Winter says he hasn't heard a single comment from a chief executive of another copper company.

THE DAY A BUSINESS JET TAUGHT
THE SHISHMAREF FIRST-GRADE CLASS.

The Citation V's unique ability to fly long distances yet land on short airstrips has allowed it to get into some pretty remote places. One such place was the tiny, isolated town of Shishmaref, near the Arctic Circle.

When the Citation landed on a narrow snowplowed strip, children came running from the nearby school. They'd never seen a jet before.

And chances are, they may never see any others besides Citations. Unless Shishmaref builds a runway long enough for less versatile business jets to use.

THE SENSIBLE CITATIONS

Cessna
A Textron Company

Chapter Three

BANISHING THE BOSSES

Participative management is the trendiest thing in organizational theory these days. In this case, trendy is also smart. The oldest and most thoroughly tested set of techniques in the productivity revolution, participative management works. Applied properly, as at Magma and Titeflex, it will lower costs, improve quality, eliminate unnecessary layers of management, and improve morale. And although it isn't essential to other techniques like factory redesign and reengineering, it reinforces and makes those changes more effective.

As used in this volume, participative management subsumes a number of complementary and overlapping concepts, including work teams, high-performance workplaces, and worker empowerment. The term encompasses a continuum of practices that start with modest employee-involvement programs and build to factories where workers manage themselves. Participative management fosters commitment by giving workers significantly more responsibility, more difficult and engaging jobs, and more autonomy over how they do those jobs. Committed workers are in turn more responsible, pay closer attention to quality, and are forever finding new ways to use materials and machines more effectively. In short, they are superproductive.

Many companies say they are changing the way they manage employees, but few are doing anything substantial. In some cases companies have experimented successfully with participative management in one or two factories but haven't implemented the system throughout the organization. Others have adopted modest employee-involvement programs but have not taken the subsequent steps toward letting employees manage themselves. The American Society for Training and Development estimates that in 1992 only 2 percent of the labor force toiled in high-performance workplaces. Edward Lawler III, a professor at the University of Southern California and one of the originators of participative-management techniques, estimates that perhaps 500 U.S. factories have been organized this way. In a $6 trillion economy, that's barely noticeable.

If participative management works so well, why are so few companies using it? Because few chief executives have gotten personally involved in implementing the change. Participative management terrifies many middle managers, and with good reason. Many will lose their jobs as the techniques become widely applied. At the least, the system forces managers to surrender a large measure of their authority and handle subordinates in new ways, a prospect few managers find appealing. So they will sabotage it unless the change is forcefully managed from the top down. "Middle managers who pilot this in large corporations end up being very unpopular," says Jon Simpson. "Some very good people have lost their jobs for succeeding [with participative-management programs]."

Motorola's experiences vividly illustrate the difficulties in converting an organization to participative management—and the astounding potential of the system. Motorola is one of the first and largest companies to adopt participative management wholesale. Former chairman Robert Galvin began the change to a participative structure in 1979. At the time, many organizational experts believed such a system would work only in factories using process technologies, such as chemical, paint, and food plants, and not on high-speed assembly lines or in offices. Some also assumed that the technique worked only in new facilities, not in existing ones with established cultures.

Galvin refused to accept those presumed limits, and he ordered Motorola's personnel department to set up a training program with the dual goals of introducing participative management and im-

1989

Although participative management has made Motorola's comeback the stuff of legend, senior managers fought the new system until former chief executive Robert W. Galvin "encouraged" their conversion.

◆

proving quality tenfold in five years. He recognized that Motorola's assembly workers needed more skills to bring company quality up to that of the Japanese.

Motorola's success has become the stuff of legend in the years since, but it wasn't easy. Early on, Motorola discovered that the training paid off only in the plants where senior managers supported the program. By 1984 the company concluded that it had to offer the training to its top managers. But the folks at the top didn't attend until Galvin himself "encouraged" them to take the course. Now annual training is mandatory for everyone in the company. The results have been outstanding, especially in the cellular telephone and paging device operations, which were the first to make the change.

Motorola University, as the company rather grandly calls its training center, has carried the participative-management gospel throughout the company, with varying degrees of success. The experiences of one group in the Tactical Electronics Division (TED) demonstrate how participative management can transform a troubled operation. They also show how tough it can be to enforce these reforms, even in a company that seems committed to change.

TED is part of Motorola's Government Electronics Group in Scottsdale, Arizona, and as the name implies, is a defense contractor. In the mid-1980s it won a Navy contract to convert 714 Sidewinder missiles from their original air-to-air configuration to an air-to-ground configuration for use against enemy radar-controlled weapons. The converted Sidewinders are called Sidearm missiles. TED's job was to take apart the 25-year-old missiles, install new guidance systems designed by the Navy, and put them back together. Simple? Yes, except that the new Sidearm guidance system has 8,000 parts and uses a lot of old-fashioned soldered wires that are much more labor-intensive (and error-prone) than printed circuits.

By the summer of 1989, TED had completed two production runs on Sidearm conversions, and both had been a mess. The assembly was plagued with high defect rates that required extensive reworking and resulted in huge work-in-process inventories, high production costs, and late deliveries. The Navy wasn't getting missiles when it wanted them, and Motorola wasn't making money on the contract. That's when Don King, the Sidearm project leader, decided to try something different. King had learned the wonders of self-directed work teams at Motorola U and wanted to try the technique on the third Sidearm run. He felt it would make a great case study because runs two and three were almost identical. Program manager A. Boyd Holmes told him to proceed.

King had a four-month break between runs two and three, so in September 1989 he put together a planning team of 25 assemblers, supervisors, and test engineers to figure out how they could build the guidance systems faster and cheaper. Holmes says he and King made a commitment to "foster total team participation, create a non-threatening, innovative atmosphere, and empower all the personnel to contribute and manage the change." Those words may sound a mite stilted, but converts to participative management really talk that way. Another frequent piece of jargon is "ownership of the process." Again the underlying thought here is that workers become much more committed when they have a role in designing the production system. Then they "own" it and have a stake in seeing that it works.

The first step in fostering the feeling of ownership was training. The design team watched motivational tapes by Tom (*In Search of Excellence*) Peters about how participative management had triumphed at other companies. Then a consultant came in to teach the group teamwork and problem-solving techniques. The team members also got instruction in basic manufacturing concepts like cycle times, flow charts, and statistical process controls.

Work teams are usually self-managing (hence the term *participative management*) in the sense that members decide among themselves who does a specific job. They sometimes set their own production schedules, do their own quality control, maintain their equipment, police absenteeism and other misbehavior by team members, do their own performance evaluations, and participate in the hiring of new employees. In this system, peer pressure and pride in work well done replace monitoring by a supervisor. If supervisors remain on the scene at all, they are there to "facilitate," to help teams solve problems. The important distinction is that these supervisors don't give orders, they give advice. The good ones always leave final decisions to team members.

Holmes and King say it was vital that they win the trust of the design team. "You have to give the team the freedom to operate, or they'll lose the enthusiasm," says King. "You can't keep them on a tether. Once the workers believed we would let them do it, they ran it." Adds Keith A. Greiner, a production supervisor on the design team and one of four "factory coordinators" during production: "When we ran into troubles, many assumed that [we] would go back to the old style of management. That didn't happen. At first we weren't sure the new autonomy was real, but the feeling of trust just grew." The factory team fell behind schedule almost immediately and was still running late in March 1990, six months into the process. Holmes and King never told their superiors. "You have to have someone running interference for the team," says King, who understood how managers might be skittish about the changes. "Management here has always been *very* top-down."

In redesigning the production floor, the planners divided it into four cells, where teams worked on subassemblies. Members of the cells were cross-trained to do each other's jobs as the need arose.

The cell structure allowed the design team to insert quality inspections at earlier production levels so that problems became apparent sooner and workers had to do fewer teardowns of completed assemblies. "We had tried cells in another plant where I was a supervisor," says Greiner. "There, we still had a lot of work-in-process inventory and reworking. The big difference was that we had walls between the cells. Workers in one cell didn't worry about what was happening in the other cells. We focused on the lack of communication when planning the third run here."

One way of focusing was a "pull" system between the cells, or what the Japanese call *kanban*. In a conventional "push" assembly line, a worker at one station does his job on a part and then pushes it to the next station. In a pull system, the guy at the first station doesn't do his work until the next station is ready to pull it from him. That allows workers to spot bottlenecks sooner, forces each cell to pay close attention to the ones ahead of and behind it, and minimizes work-in-process inventory. The designers also decided to tear down the walls of the room where test engineers did their quality inspections and to cut the number of inspectors from 10 to five. The test engineers were the only group that chafed under the new system. Some were miffed that "lowly" assemblers were now doing their job, but they seemed even more put out about losing their "clubhouse," says King. "They weren't elite anymore."

The design team made three other important changes. One was rewriting the assembly instructions, which presented information in a haphazard fashion and were hard to interpret. The team put the rewritten instructions on personal computers around the floor so that workers could quickly pull up a specific operation on the screen, with an image of the assembly involved and the wiring instructions marked and described step by step. The new instructions not only reduced errors, but also simplified assembly so much that materials handling was cut in half.

The second change was adding a parts storeroom adjacent to the production floor. Normal procedure at the Government Electronics Group is to keep parts in a central stockroom. The design team concluded that this required too much notice of which parts would be needed on a given day. Adding a local stockroom enabled the Sidearm team to order parts from suppliers just a week ahead instead of the normal lead time of several months and to move parts to the production floor daily. That simple change saved nearly $150,000 in payroll costs alone. Finally, the design team decided to keep all the parts from a disassembled missile together on the logical—and correct—assumption that parts from the same missile would go back together more easily.

When it came time to assemble the full crew of 50 production workers (culled from elsewhere within TED), the design team made the selections itself, a common practice in participative management. The team interviewed prospective members and put them in problem-solving situations to see how well they worked with others. Holmes says about half the prospects either didn't pass muster or didn't want to be part of the team. "The workers they did bring on knew more about this project in a day," he says, "than they knew about others they had worked on for 18 months."

The Sidearm workers functioned as a bona fide self-managed team when production began. Says King, sounding like a man whose son has just made Eagle Scout: "One of my litmus tests for how this was working was the number of decisions I had to make, and that was virtually none. I expected that some people would be coming to me all the time, but they never did." Adds Greiner: "In the early phases I got a lot of questions. But two or three months into the program something happened. [The workers] resolved problems or issues themselves and told me about it after the fact." Greiner also says that the assemblers didn't always hew to the design team's plan. "We followed the plan as a guideline," he says. "But we kept our flexibility and built on people's ideas."

How managers handle disagreement between themselves and their teams can derail a participative organization or make it a standout success. If facilitators seem to arbitrarily veto subordinates' decisions, workers lose faith in the system, become uninvolved, and stop contributing ideas and extra efforts. The better way, experts say, is to give workers their head. If a change is wrong, the team will quickly recognize the error and reverse course. And often, ideas that initially seem dumb to supervisors turn out to be right.

The improvements in the next run of Sidearm were greater than King had hoped. Since the previous runs had been late, King told the team he wanted the last one completed by November 1990, five months ahead of the scheduled delivery date. The team said it could finish the job by September and did. In run two, King had needed two overlapping 10-hour shifts, as well as considerable weekend overtime, to get the job done. On run three, the Sidearm team used one

SHORTLY AFTER FLYING IN A CITATION, HUNDREDS OF PASSENGERS HAVE GONE ON TO BECOME CELEBRATED SPORTS HEROES.

In 1987 and again in 1991, hundreds of Citation owners volunteered their aircraft, pilots and fuel to airlift thousands of athletes to the International Special Olympics Games. The airlift was organized by Cessna. But the generous cooperation of Citation owners brought it to reality.

When we asked Citation owners to help these special people celebrate life in an unforgettable way, they didn't think twice.

They did it twice.

THE SENSIBLE CITATIONS

Cessna
A Textron Company

eight-hour shift and little overtime. The crew on run two never managed to sustain a production rate of 10 units a week; the team on run three put out 13 units a week. Quantum improvements were evident in every measure of production efficiency. Direct labor hours per unit dropped 32 percent. The number of defects per unit (the cause of all the reworking on earlier runs) dropped 75 percent, work-in-process inventory was down 71 percent, the production rate was 63 percent higher, and pick cycles (the time to get parts to the floor) dropped 93 percent. The cycle time from parts availability to shipment fell 53 percent.

Motorola revels in its triumphs. Ralph Love, the vice-president and general manager in charge of TED, worked the line one day, and the company made an 18-minute videotape about the wonders the team had achieved. The workers loved it. "The assemblers, the ones who have to build [the missiles], were being listened to," says Greiner. "There was more to the success than bottom-line profit."

And less. Although the Sidearm team was a great success, its changes didn't last. After the contract was complete, the team members dispersed to other projects in the sprawling Scottsdale complex. Most of them went back to the old style of managing, because few of the project leaders or program managers seem as enlightened about participative management as King and Holmes. Several program managers told their employees that they couldn't even watch the Sidearm video. "The members of the team are now spread through the division, trying to initiate this from the floor up, but they are running into roadblocks," says King. "Many have left the company because they had to go back to the old way of working and didn't want that anymore."

As the fate of the Sidearm team suggests, the biggest stumbling block in changing to participative management is managers, not workers. That's hardly a surprise. The changes this brings in the lives of workers are all pleasant: more interesting jobs, more freedom, more opportunities to think and innovate, and a whole lot less confrontation. Most workers are quick to embrace this system—once they become convinced that the changes are real and not just another charade to trick them into working harder.

Managers and supervisors, on the other hand, have plenty to fear. Most of all, you're asking them to give up a system they trust for this new, seemingly loony idea. What's more, factories and offices using participative management normally have flat organizational structures with few layers of management. Many have only three supervisory levels: team leaders, department heads, and the boss. Eliminating unnecessary levels of monitoring and control is an important source of the cost savings from participative management. Hence, shop foremen and middle managers have to worry about losing their jobs.

Passing power and control to lower levels in the organization obviously threatens the status of everyone who has power now. In many cases that threat is manifested in the egalitarian trappings of participatively managed facilities. They have no reserved parking for the bosses, no separate management dining rooms, and Spartan offices. Those superficial changes may sound unimportant, but the rank and file love them, and psychologists say it is important in this system to break down symbolic barriers between managers and workers.

Managers instinctively see such changes as damaging even if their pay is unaffected. For those high enough to be making decisions about how the place is run, changing the management style carries the implicit message that what they have been doing is wrong—and their fault. When a manager says participative techniques won't work in his plant or department because it is somehow "different," what he usually means is, "It's not my fault that we haven't done this already. It's the environment."

Moving from control to commitment, as participative-management expert Dick Walton calls it, creates another kind of uncertainty for managers and supervisors. They have to unlearn their old controlling behavior and assume new roles that, at least at the outset, are ambiguous and require skills they probably don't have. As Walton observes, facilitating requires interpersonal skills and conceptual abilities that autocratic shop foremen often lack. Managers higher up the ladder are being asked to learn a new set of skills that may have limited value in the job market. If participative management is simply an experiment in a single plant, those skills may have limited value even within their own company. And as Jon Simpson of Titeflex says, a successful experiment can jeopardize their careers.

How do you persuade managers to implement what may be their own demise? The answer is that you give them no choice. The basic message has to be: "This is the way we will operate from now on. Those who embrace the new system will prosper. Those who resist will not be here." The CEO has to carry through and see to it that everyone gets into line, as did Burgess Winter at Magma and Simpson at Titeflex. Otherwise, attempting a change to a participative system is pointless.

Experts in participative management agree that beyond laying down the law, the best answer to the problem of management resistance is intensive training for supervisors and managers before effecting any changes. This usually starts with instruction on the theory of participative management and team dynamics followed by a lot of talk about "changing the paradigm." In this context the paradigm is the predominant behavioral model and the assumptions behind it (as in, workers are lazy and unreliable, so foremen must see to it that the work gets done). After learning the new paradigm (we're all in this together, and facilitators are here to offer suggestions and help conscientious workers grow), supervisors go through role-playing exercises to practice the new techniques.

Consultants who have trained supervisors and managers say their students start out suspicious and resistant to change. But as they begin to see the possibilities in the new system, most become accepting, if not downright enthusiastic. That seems only natural. Who, after all, wouldn't prefer to work in an environment characterized by a spirit of cooperation and commitment to shared goals? The trick is to get employees to believe it will happen and that they will do at least as well as they have under the old regime. In situations in which many management and supervisory positions will become redundant, that trick can be accomplished only by identifying the people who support change and eliminating the rest.

Companies in a broad spectrum of industries have proved that participative management can work anywhere—on assembly lines, in offices, in service industries. It can work as well in established facilities as it does in new plants. Ford made it work on the Taurus. Irving W. Bailey II, chief executive of Capital Holding, a diversified financial services company in Louisville, Kentucky, is making it work there. However, the experts do not have a proven recipe for getting it right. What works in one place might not in another; participative management has to be tailored to each company. Most experts believe a gradual approach is easier on everyone and may be more profitable in the long run than going cold turkey. The problem is figuring out how to make the transition. Unfortunately, it appears that most companies start out with a token effort at employee involvement, often in the form of quality circles, and then never follow through.

One company that did follow through from tentative employee-involvement programs to full-blown worker management is Helene Curtis. The changes there are the work of Robert Sack, the company's vice-president of operations. At Helene Curtis, operations includes all manufacturing and distribution. In the early 1980s, chief executive Ronald J. Gidwitz, the grandson of the founder, decided the cosmetics company had to grow 15 to 20 percent annually to escape the ranks of the also-ran. Sack had the daunting prospect of accommodating that growth without any meaningful expansion of the company's ancient factory. The 80-year-old five-story building on Chicago's west side is "so antiquated that it shouldn't work at all," says consultant Richard H. Axelrod of Wilmette, Illinois.

Helene Curtis has always been a paternalistic employer, an attribute that enabled it to stave off two unions' attempts to organize the employees in the 1970s. That style suited Sack, who comes across as an uncommonly benevolent manager. In 1984 he turned to employee-involvement programs as a way to boost productivity while preserving the paternalism. One gets the impression that Sack also saw employee involvement as a means of treating workers the way he believes they should be treated. Sack and his lieutenants visited companies with participative-management programs and saw nothing that seemed to fit Helene Curtis's circumstances, so they decided to improvise.

Sack hired Axelrod to conduct focus-group interviews with Helene Curtis workers, who said they wanted to contribute to the company's growth but felt their ideas did not get a fair hearing. Those findings led to the creation of problem-solving groups of managers, supervisors, and workers from various departments (what Sack calls both a vertical and horizontal cut). One group suggested a new layout for a shampoo bottling line that improved speed and quality while reducing maintenance and accidents. Another group designed a recreation center for the manufacturing plant. The biggest impact the problem-solving groups had was on morale. Workers loved the chance to interact with managers as collaborators rather than subordinates.

Within a couple of years, however, the groups had become bureaucratic. In effect, they were a parallel organization within the

THE U.S. LEADER
ELECTED BY THE ENTIRE WORLD.

Of all the business jet choices today, one line is the undisputed leader. One is chosen by more companies than any other.

Before choosing, most companies carefully evaluated several candidates. They looked at overall performance and operating cost. They compared safety records. Reliability. Cabin comfort. And support networks.

Then companies in 49 U.S. states and in 58 other nations all arrived at the same sensible conclusion. They all bought Cessna Citations.

THE SENSIBLE CITATIONS

Cessna
A Textron Company

operations division, with a planning committee to set direction, a steering committee to form and oversee the problem-solving groups, and facilitators to train and assist workers. Supervisors complained that all the bureaucracy slowed results. Sack then tried "action teams." Anyone could start an action team simply by identifying a problem and recruiting people to work on it. Unlike the problem-solving groups, individual action teams lasted only as long as it took to complete an assignment.

By 1988 Sack and Axelrod were looking for ways to make participative management an integral part of day-to-day operations instead of something that happened on the side. One problem was that employees liked the action teams but viewed them as separate from "work." Another was that they involved only 20 to 30 percent of the staff. Step three, which began in 1988, was an experiment with self-managed work teams. One went to work on the organization of a new distribution center going up a couple of blocks from the manufacturing plant. The other redesigned the company's largest shampoo bottling line. Sack says workers were surprised and pleased that he gave them control of the biggest bottling line. Each team consisted of a supervisor and workers with a cross section of skills. "We asked for volunteers," says Sack. "If we got more than one for a given slot, we had the other team members sort it out, not us."

Sack got an immediate demonstration of what teams can achieve. The bottling team redesigned the line in a way that was radically different from the rest of the plant. Workers do their own routine maintenance and quality inspection, and they are all in a single job classification called production technician. The team put the workers on a pay-for-knowledge system: they get raises as they learn more jobs on the line. It also requires that everyone have a high-school or general equivalency diploma. "Now we offer a GED course, which we didn't do before," says Sack.

The company learned that Chesebrough-Pond's was introducing Rave shampoo to compete with Helene Curtis's successful Salon Selectives. Helene Curtis decided to counterpunch by cramming store shelf space with Salon Selectives and its Suave shampoo. Sack told the workers what was coming and what they needed to do. From June through August 1988, production changed from two eight-hour shifts to two 12-hour ones, and from five days a week to seven. Volunteers filled the weekend slots, so Sack didn't have to press anyone into duty. The strategy worked as planned, and Sack still smiles when he recalls the experience. "It gave us a feeling that there are mountains you can climb together," he says. "Teams accomplish more than we thought was possible."

Meanwhile, the team planning the move to the new highly automated distribution center was stalled. "There were some frustrations in getting their arms around moving," says Sack. "The project was just too big. We hadn't learned that you shouldn't give teams an assignment that is too large." The team finally decided to hold off on job redesign until after the move, although it did recommend some changes to the building. Helene Curtis got an immediate 40 percent savings in unit costs when the new distribution center replaced six old warehouses, but Sack and Howard Wagner, then the head of distribution, figure that was mostly from the new, more efficient equipment. Productivity has continued to improve about 20 percent annually since then, which both men credit to the work teams' eventual redesign of jobs at the center.

The redesign signaled the start of real progress, Wagner says; the team began looking at the organization of the center and its objectives rather than at specific functions. "The distribution center was set up by functions—forklifts, the office, et cetera—in order to have a thumb on each function and for accounting purposes," he says. "That doesn't even address what the organization is trying to accomplish." Wagner characterizes the redesign process as a way of changing the organization chart so that people can work together to eliminate problems more easily.

In the case of the center, Wagner's crew redefined the purpose of the operation. "We had designed the distribution center to get things in and get them out," he says. "But as a service, our job doesn't end with shipping but when the bill is paid. So now we track goods until they get to the customers and [we] settle any disputes. The post-shipping group is a new function for us, and the follow-up attention it gives is what creates quality as perceived by the customer." Helene Curtis's customers apparently perceive a lot of quality. In the last few years, the company has become a regular recipient of vendor awards from Wal-Mart and K Mart.

By the time it was through, the design team had completely reorganized the center. In the process, it abolished the administrative office. "When the team looked at the distribution center as a system, it discovered that the office did not have a purpose," says Wagner. "It was not a natural team. People were classified as 'office' just because they worked at a desk." What had been a conventional organization with eight departments is now a group of six teams: administration, planning, order filling, loading trucks, equipment control, and post shipping. Each team is made up of employees who must work together daily to accomplish a process.

Once the teams were formed, they sat down and negotiated what they would do for each other, when, and at what level of quality. "In the process," says Wagner, "we discovered we were doing many things that nobody wanted." Now each team focuses on quality and on serving its "customer," whether that is a retail chain or another team within the company. "Teams have to be focused," says Wagner, who now runs manufacturing. "They have to know the object of the game. It is quite an education to get everyone to understand his internal and external customers." The emphasis on customers is a way of channeling each worker's thoughts toward improving service and reducing waste, an orientation that often proves more effective than dealing directly with costs or productivity. In fact, cost is only Sack's fourth priority, after quality, customer service, and flexibility.

The flexibility extends to the way Helene Curtis organizes teams. "We want continuity from plant to plant, but each operation must have its own individuality," says Sack. Several years ago, for example, Sack got the chance to buy a small plastic-bottle factory. Until then Helene Curtis had "decorated" (printed the labels on) its plastic bottles but had not made them. Sack picked five employees with an assortment of management skills to decide whether the company could master the bottle technology. The committee concluded that the company should go ahead with the project, both to learn how to make bottles and as a laboratory to learn more about teams. The committee also decided to recruit workers from within Helene Curtis instead of hiring employees of the former factory owner.

Mike Kamowski, the manager of the bottle plant, says his design team was "really naive," but in this case inexperience doesn't seem to have been a serious problem. Helene Curtis recaptured its entire investment in the bottle plant in just 18 months, and the 100 employees at the small plant can turn out 100 million plastic bottles a year.

Kamowski didn't want separate departments in the new operation because he believed they would lead to hierarchy and bureaucracy. Instead the design team listed all the functions needed within the plant and created a progression of skills for workers to learn. Then it organized all but four of the 100 employees in the bottle plant into teams. (The exceptions are people who do single-person jobs like purchasing.) But instead of setting up teams the way they are in the distribution center, Kamowski and company organized them according to function. Everyone involved in bottle molding on a shift is on one team, for example, whereas everyone in bottle decorating on a shift makes up another team.

The experimental team on the big bottling line and the ones in the distribution center and bottle factory proved so effective that in 1991 Sack decided to reorganize all 1,200 employees in the operations division into teams. Once the teams were established, Sack let them redesign their own work cells and reassign people to different jobs within the cell. "A lot of teams intuitively recognize that some individuals are better at certain jobs," says Sack. "Workers accept those judgments if their peers make them, but they won't if a supervisor decides."

Over the years Sack and Axelrod occasionally held meetings with rank-and-file workers and regular sessions with managers and supervisors to brief them on what was happening. They also put managers and supervisors through workshops to get them to question whether they were providing the right role models for workers. "The workshops let managers see how they can work with their peers in different ways," says Axelrod. The workshops led to the creation of a participative-management committee made up of all the department heads within the operations division to oversee the transition. To make sure his managers' hearts were in the right place, Sack included support of cultural change in their performance appraisals. In 1992 he added "upward" evaluations of managers by subordinates.

After eight years of experimenting, Sack is convinced he chose the right course. His challenge—accommodating Helene Curtis's growth—made the job easier and more pleasant than it might have been. "I didn't have to worry about laying off supervisors," he says. "They do different things now, but I could keep them, because we were growing." Still, the operations work force has grown only about half as fast as sales, and many of the new bodies are in support functions, not in the factory. "We did this with a certain amount of faith that it was the right thing to do," says Sack. And the profitable thing as well.

THE MEN WHO MANAGE CESSNA AIRCRAFT COMPANY HAVE HAD ONE THING IN COMMON EVER SINCE THEY WERE BOYS.

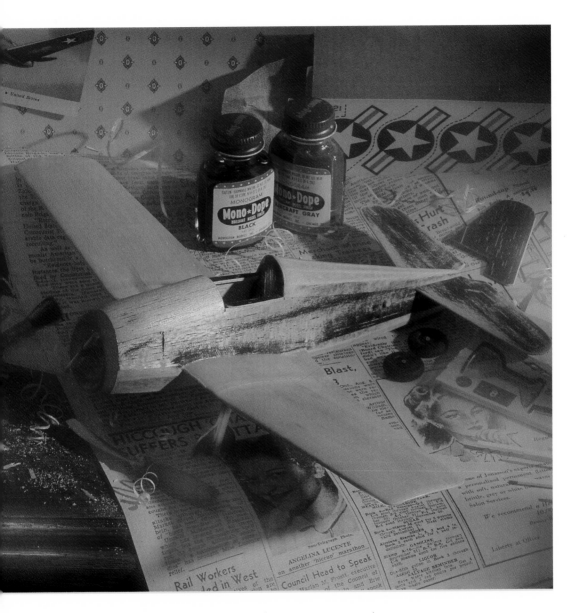

You could call it a lifelong fascination with aviation. You might even call it an obsession. Whatever it is, Cessna's top executives have never outgrown it. All of them are active pilots.

Some would say you don't have to be a pilot to build a good airplane. And they're probably right. But to build a great airplane, we believe it takes something beyond mere aerodynamics and aluminum.

We believe it takes a little passion.

THE SENSIBLE CITATIONS

Cessna
A Textron Company

Chapter Four

MANUFACTURING MAGIC

Jack F. Reichert has an uncommon affection for the sport of bowling, which isn't terribly surprising. He has been with Brunswick Corporation for more than 35 years, the last 11 as chief executive. Bowling has been with Brunswick forever. "Bowling is at the core of our business," says Reichert, who spent his first 14 years with the company in its bowling and billiards division. "Bowling provided the cash to go into boats, fishing, and everything else we've done." Not so long ago, however, Brunswick's bowling business was consuming cash instead of providing it, and that presented a major problem.

Brunswick gets the largest share of its more than $2 billion in annual revenues from its four boat divisions, but most of the world still thinks of it as a bowling company. And Reichert's fondness for the division where he began made it only natural to fix the bowling business rather than shutter, sell, or spin it off to shareholders. The manner in which his subordinates revived the division—and the bowling-ball business in particular—is a direct result of Reichert's unusual style of leadership. It's a graphic example of the productivity improvements companies can achieve with what is called just-in-time manufacturing.

Just-in-time, or JIT for short, is Japan's most valuable export to the U.S., but too few American companies have been buying this particular product. To be sure, just about every company says it now uses JIT inventory controls, the Japanese technique that came into vogue in the U.S. in the 1970s. The practice of ordering components and raw materials so that they arrive "just in time" to be used in production reduces the need for working capital to finance inventories. However, JIT inventory management is only part of the JIT manufacturing system. In its totality, JIT is a radically different way of organizing factories—a different philosophy of production—that routinely boosts productivity by 30 and sometimes more than 50 percent. Used properly, its proponents say, JIT can also foster continuing productivity gains of 10 percent a year. And the technique called reengineering, which can be thought of as a sort of second-generation JIT, can achieve the same kind of results or better in service businesses and support functions.

1989

CEO Jack F. Reichert led the successful redesign of Brunswick's bowling-ball factories.

Put most simply, JIT is the application of just-in-time principles to every aspect of production. Companies order parts and materials to arrive as close as possible to the time they will be used. Workers at the beginning of the production process do not make a component until the next group is ready to use it in a subassembly. That group doesn't make subassemblies until the next is ready to do the final assembly, and final assembly doesn't happen until it is time to ship the goods. Thus, everything in the production chain happens just in time to get the goods out the door. When companies operate this way, they can get by with much smaller inventories of raw materials, less work-in-process inventory, smaller warehouses of finished goods, and a whole lot less equipment and support personnel to transport and track all that stuff. Those ancillary savings, more than reductions in direct labor, make JIT so successful.

JIT, which was introduced to the U.S. by productivity gurus like Wickham Skinner, has been winning converts for more than 15 years, but it hasn't permeated the fabric of American business. Andersen Consulting, one of the leading proselytizers of the JIT religion, estimates that fewer than 15 percent of U.S. factories have switched to the system, which means that the vast majority of companies are passing up an opportunity to get greater efficiency and much lower costs with the equipment and people they already have. That so few have made the move to JIT is not surprising. After all, it is Japanese. More important, JIT requires fundamental changes in the way businesses operate. Pete Peterson of Andersen Consulting, who has advised clients around the world, observes that U.S. companies seem more resistant to change than those in Europe and Asia and that successful companies are the most resistant of all.

JIT runs counter to the way American business has organized production for nearly a century. Industrial efficiency has meant long production runs (or batch sizes) that capture economies of scale and keep machines running at full speed. Most machines are used to fashion many parts or perform multiple functions, such as a filling machine that puts peanut butter into 6-ounce, 8-ounce, and 16-ounce jars. If the changeover (or setup) time to recalibrate the machine from 6- to 16-ounce jars is long, the conventional solution is to do long runs of 6-ounce jars before changing to 16-ounce. That minimizes the amount of downtime between batches and increases machine use, a frequently used measure of productivity. But long runs also create the need for extra forklifts to move the large batches of goods to and from storage, the storage space itself, the people to run the forklifts and warehouses, and unnecessary inventories. JIT has proven that, at least in today's world, long production runs are less efficient, not more. Hence, JIT practitioners look for ways to reduce changeover times.

The essence of JIT is simplicity—making everything in the production process, from product design to final assembly, as uncomplicated as possible. As Pete Peterson explains it, "The Japanese put more money in designing processes in their plants, while we throw dollars at automation. We have a new-gear fixation, while the Japanese orientation is to simplify." When factories and machines become big and complex, Peterson says, specialization and centralization run rampant and overhead soars. Consider, for example, that on average U.S. manufacturers employ twice as much indirect labor as their Japanese counterparts. A U.S. Department of Defense survey in the mid-1980s found that Japanese manufacturers had four support people (for example, salesmen, order clerks, warehousemen, accountants, managers) for each employee directly involved in production. The ratio for U.S. manufacturers is eight to one. Result: even when the U.S. companies are way ahead in production efficiency, they can lose to Japanese competitors that are ahead of them in total efficiency.

The first thing you notice when you enter a JIT factory is how different it looks from an ordinary one. For one thing, JIT manufacturing requires considerably less space. When the Jacobs Vehicle Equipment Company in Bloomfield, Connecticut, converted to JIT several years ago, it freed up enough space to put in ping-pong tables and basketball and volleyball courts for employees. Second, JIT factories are organized differently. Instead of grouping similar machines, which is the norm in conventional plants, JIT facilities are broken up into factories within a factory. This organization arises from the insight that smaller factories, which have more direct and immediate interaction between workers and fewer support personnel to administer complexity, are more efficient than larger ones. Think of the difference this way: designing, administering, and scheduling the factories within a factory is somewhat like planning a series of commando raids instead of mounting the invasion of Normandy.

Most of the factories within a factory are work cells, each containing the different types of machines needed to make similar parts or subassemblies. In a cell, a part moves from one machine to another until it is complete and then moves on to an adjacent cell for the next step. In a conventional plant, where machines and work are grouped by type, a part will go to one area to have one operation performed and then wait, sometimes for weeks, to be transported to another area for the next operation. That's where all the work-in-process (WIP) inventory comes from. Cells squeeze out those delays, speeding the work flow and eliminating unnecessary inventory and handling costs. To shorten the distance parts travel, cells are typically clustered around the final assembly line. If one cell supplies parts or subassemblies to several others, it lies closest to the one that uses more of its output than the others.

The cell arrangement has several advantages beyond savings on WIP and materials handling. If the workers in one cell have misadjusted a machine and are producing faulty components, workers in the next cell often spot the problem right away. In a conventional plant producing large batches, parts sit for days or weeks before moving on to the next step. As a result, the workers on the misadjusted machine might turn out thousands, even hundreds of thousands, of defective parts before anyone notices. Cells also make it easier—indeed, essential—to train workers to perform multiple tasks. In addition to making their work more interesting, this multiskilling gives workers a better understanding of the product, makes them more sensitive to quality, and, in the best situations, kindles a spirit of entrepreneurship among workers and managers. You will have noted by now that cells play a big part in both JIT and participative management. That isn't a conspiracy. The folks who developed the techniques arrived at cells for subtly different reasons, but the outcome is the same: cells and work teams are more efficient.

The superior wisdom of JIT is most evident in its achievements. Experts on the subject say companies switching to JIT can expect to reduce space needs by 50 percent, allowing companies to lease out unused space, close some factories and consolidate production in others, expand capacity without adding new buildings—or put in a basketball court. Inventories of raw materials and finished goods typically drop almost 75 percent, while WIP nearly vanishes. When industrial engineers focus on improving machine setup procedures, they can cut changeover times by 75 percent. Similarly, workers in cells often do their own maintenance on equipment, cutting machine downtime by as much as 75 percent. Most impressive of all, JIT factories routinely produce 90 percent fewer defects than they did before they were redesigned.

JIT seems especially well suited to the 1990s, when speed is becoming an ever more important facet of competition. Companies that get products to market sooner and then respond faster to customer orders have a huge advantage over their competitors. That will be increasingly true for consumer-products companies as more and more retailers emulate Wal-Mart's system of just-in-time ordering. When a shopper buys an item at a Wal-Mart store, the purchase is automatically recorded in the company's computer, which in turn transmits the information to suppliers' computers, telling them when and where to deliver a replacement. To respond best to those types of systems, a manufacturer has to have flexible factories with small batch sizes. Time has also become more important in industrial goods, as Titeflex belatedly discovered (see Chapter Two), and in services.

Indeed, some consultants use speed as the main selling feature of JIT techniques. The Boston Consulting Group calls its product time-based competition, whereas Andersen Consulting sells "time-compression management." Pete Peterson, who coined the latter phrase, says, "I have never seen a company that didn't prosper after it reduced the time to manufacture its product." Peterson and others also point out that speed and flexibility enable companies to be market-driven: they can respond much more opportunistically to changes in demand when freed from long lead times.

Time-compression doesn't work by getting employees to do their jobs faster. Instead it involves finding the sources of delays and

PERHAPS THE MOST IMPORTANT THING WE BUILD AT THIS CESSNA PLANT IS HUMAN POTENTIAL.

A year ago, this Cessna worker was considered unemployable. Lacking skills and education, she and her children lived on welfare checks.

But a new program, initiated by Cessna Aircraft Company, changed all that. The program provides job training for the undereducated. It gives each person a basic skill, a means to make a living, and a source of pride.

Graduates of the program now build high-quality parts for Cessna and, at the same time, something even more valuable. Better lives for themselves.

THE SENSIBLE CITATIONS

Cessna
A Textron Company

eliminating them. Hurry-up-and-wait has become the norm in American business—from motorcycle manufacturing to health insurance. "In a manufacturing plant, a part typically spends 90 percent of its time waiting for the next step in the process," says Peterson. JIT experts exorcise the waiting time by rethinking production processes and also by doing a lot of old-fashioned tinkering with machines and product designs. This tinkering has a long tradition in American business, but one that in recent decades has often been lost or put aside. Harley-Davidson Motor Company, for example, makes two crankshafts designed by separate teams of engineers. The crankshafts used to have different angles for the oil access holes. When the company redesigned one so that the angle of the hole was the same as the other, it cut the changeover time on the drilling machine from 114 minutes to 12. Little things like that add up to a lot of time and a lot of dollars.

When Peterson begins a project, his goal is to reduce the cycle time by 90 percent. Cycle time refers to the duration of a process, such as the number of days from an order's arrival at a factory until the goods are shipped. Several years ago, for example, Steelcase hired Peterson to compress the time it takes to fill orders for office desks at its Grand Rapids, Michigan, factory. At the time, Steelcase was getting desks out in 25 days. That was the fastest cycle time in the industry, Peterson says, but Steelcase wanted to shorten it to 20 days. Peterson stunned his client by saying it should shoot for two days—one to make the components and one to assemble and ship the desks. "They laughed," he says, "but we did get it down to four days."

Which brings us back to bowling balls. Brunswick's bowling and billiards division came on hard times in 1980 and lost money in five of the next six years. Luckily for the division, Jack Reichert ascended to the company's top spot in April 1982. His predecessors had been devoted to strong central control and insisted that all important decisions be made at the Skokie, Illinois, headquarters. "We had 14 division presidents and four group VPs, all in Skokie," he says. Reichert was the sole exception to the rule when he ran the Marine Power Group (Mercury outboards) in Fond du Lac, Wisconsin. "My boss kept insisting that I move to Skokie, but I told him there was no need, that I could be there in two hours whenever he really needed me. A couple weeks later I got a call to report to Skokie immediately. I got in a plane and made it there in an hour and 40 minutes. He didn't want to see me. He just wanted to test whether I could respond as fast as I had promised."

Reichert finally made the move to Skokie in 1977 as president of the company. When he became CEO five years later, he insisted that almost everyone else leave headquarters. In Reichert's view, operating decisions should be made in the operating divisions. "Corporate bodies do not create wealth," he says. "Operating divisions do. The job of corporate is to reinvest and preserve what the divisions create." Reichert promptly eliminated the position of chief operating officer, retired the four group executives, and consolidated 11 divisions (four had been sold) into eight, all reporting to him. As part of his plan to move decisions back to the divisions, he increased the capital spending authority of the division presidents from $25,000 to $250,000. Says Reichert: "Under the old system there was no sense of ownership of investments because too many people had to sign off on them. If something did not work out, the division president could rightly point to 10 others who had participated in and approved the decision. By eliminating the signoffs, I gave ownership and entrepreneurship to the divisions. Then I had to push them to spend their new capital authority." They eventually got the knack.

Reichert's restructuring of top management, which coincided with an unprecedented boom in boat sales, paid off. In less than six years, Brunswick's stock split 8-for-1 and rose 18-fold (from $13.125 to $240 a share, adjusted for the split). Even after a washout in boats (industry sales fell 60 percent from their 1988 peak, Brunswick's 44 percent), the company's stock was nine times as high in 1992 as when Reichert took over. But while the boat business boomed, bowling slid along in the gutter. Among other problems, Brunswick simply wasn't smart about the way it manufactured bowling equipment. That is, not until David Bloomfield, then director of manufacturing at the division and now head of capital-equipment products, began redesigning Brunswick's factories in Muskegon, Michigan, and in Europe.

The jazz in the bowling business is in pinsetters, ball returns, and the automatic scoring systems that Brunswick makes, but the salesmen like to have pins and balls in their kit when they call on customers. Bloomfield tackled Brunswick's pin factory first, but to no avail. He made the plant more efficient, but Brunswick's pins were still inferior to those made with a superior coating by Vulcan International. So Brunswick closed its pin factory and formed a joint venture with Vulcan. The balls, however, still roll out of Muskegon, profitable again after a decade of losses.

Bowling balls come in two basic varieties. The cheap ones are polyester; the pros and serious amateurs use balls made of urethane. The first step in making a ball is molding a core of resin, sandstone, and a lightweight filler used to vary the weight. Robots grind the cores to uniform size and symmetry, and then they go to a casting room where the polyester or urethane cover is poured over the core in a mold. After the cover cures, workers grind the balls again and engrave the serial number and logo with a computer-driven laser. Then the balls get a final grinding and polishing. When Dave Bloomfield began to redesign the ball plant in 1988, it took five to 13 days (13 to 24 shifts) to make a ball. Today it takes less than 24 hours, and most of that is for the cores and covers to harden. The only part of the operation that remains the same is the core molding, which the company had retooled in the mid-1980s. The changes came in casting and finishing.

In the old days, cores came out of molding and embarked on a journey along an assembly line organized by the various processes. First they went to a casting group, then to grinding, then to laser engraving, then to bronzing (filling the engraved logo with resin of a contrasting color), then to another grinding machine, and finally on to buffing and packaging. Along the way, defective balls moved off the main line and onto a rework line; most of the flaws were cosmetic. "We sometimes had more on the rework line than on the line to finished goods," says Bloomfield. By the time it arrived at a shipping box, a ball had traveled anywhere from 900 to 4,600 feet. From that point it probably went to a warehouse. Brunswick was making balls in batches that averaged around 1,000 and went as high as 2,500. With bowling balls, a batch is a lot of the same type and color. Mixing large amounts of resin at the same time seemed the most efficient way to cast the covers.

Bloomfield called in Pete Peterson and his crew at Andersen Consulting to help with the redesign. The first emphasis was on quality. Mistakes were pushing too many balls onto the rework line, and enough cosmetic flaws slipped through to hurt Brunswick's reputation. Another problem was air bubbles in the cores, which required costly manual patching. The consultants changed the method of mixing resins so that they contained less air and retooled the nozzles that pour resin into the molds to eliminate most of the remaining air. Brunswick also got major results from minor changes in the way it mixes resins for casting the outer skin. At Andersen's suggestion it switched to smaller mixing tanks and installed electronic metering equipment to control the amounts of resins and pigments. Larry Lienesch, the general manager of the plant, says that reduced the number of flaws and enabled him to cut the batch size to 65 balls.

The most significant changes came in the finishing operation. Brunswick ripped out the line with separate stations for grinding, engraving, regrinding, and polishing and replaced it with three work cells, each of which does all those jobs. The company made workers responsible for quality and taught them how to maintain their own machines. Instead of going to a rework line, imperfect balls get fixed right away in the work cells. Lienesch says Brunswick now has to rework only 2 to 3 percent of the balls, down from more than 10 percent in 1988. The company also negotiated a new compensation system with its workers, who are members of the International Association of Machinists. In the past, workers were paid a piecework rate that varied with the job they did. They still are on a piecework system, but now all the workers in a cell get the same rate. Lienesch observes that since the workers in a cell are paid as a group, they work much more cooperatively.

All the changes took less than two years and produced the usual impressive results. Bloomfield cut the floor space in the ball plant by 50 percent, which allowed him to close another building and move bowling-alley fabrication into the newly vacant ball space. The distance from molding through packaging is now only 450 feet. And inventories are down 85 percent. Raw materials now leave the plant as finished balls within two weeks, versus a three-month stay under the old system. Ten years ago, scrap ran as high as 20 percent of materials. Now it is budgeted at 2 percent, and the actual figure for the first half of 1992 was 1.2 percent.

Additional savings result from worker suggestions, which Brunswick solicits, implements, and posts near the cafeteria on a chart that resembles a United Way progress poster. The savings goal for 1992 was $400,000, or roughly 4 percent of costs. By July, savings were running at an annual rate of $546,000. One idea was to replace the foam pads Brunswick put at the top and bottom of bowling-ball boxes with pieces of cardboard. The savings of 8.5 cents per box on one million boxes a year adds up to $85,000. Another worker suggested using silicone gel instead of rubber "O" rings to seal the casting molds, saving $18,000 a year.

Handsome as those improvements are, they weren't enough to save the ball business by themselves. Brunswick also had to do much better in the marketplace. In 1991 the company had about 40 percent of the market in polyester balls but only 19 percent of the more profitable urethane market. Bryan Collins, a former marketing manager who now heads consumer products in the bowling and billiards division, figured that the company had to sell 50,000 more balls than the previous year's roughly 900,000 to break even in 1992. Toward the end of the year, it appeared that sales would be up by at least 100,000, with all of the increase in the high end of the market. Brunswick is doing so much better in urethane balls because it fixed the cosmetic problems and because it came out with a dynamite new ball called the Rhino Pro. The Rhino Pro, which top bowlers love for its ease of control, is the hottest thing in professional bowling and a sort of rolling testament to the value of time compression. After consulting with major customers and its resin supplier, Brunswick went from concept to production of the new ball in just four months. When the Rhino Pro went into production in May 1992, the company had to scrap just 60 balls. The number of rejects on a new ball used to be 500 or more.

The changes at the bowling and billiards division might have happened regardless of who was running things at headquarters, but they almost certainly happened sooner because of Jack Reichert's special style of leadership. Far more than most bosses, Reichert believes in giving subordinates the latitude to do their jobs as they see fit. "When you give people the authority to do a job and create a climate where they feel like owners," he says, "the result is a significant improvement in productivity and quality." Reichert is equally big on values and the impact they have on an organization. A year after he became CEO, he had written a statement of corporate values, stressing quality products, satisfying customers (the most important factor in long-term success), and instilling dignity, pride, and trust in the workers. A year later, and every year since, he has put the statement in the annual report—ahead of the financial summary. "I didn't invent the values," Reichert says. "Brunswick always had them. But I did articulate them in ways that hadn't been done before. The CEO has to articulate his own views of what is important."

Reichert also has a conviction that the boss ought to suffer along with shareholders and employees when a company comes on hard times. After the boat business tanked, and Brunswick's sales, profits, and stock price went down with it, Reichert asked the compensation committee of the board to cut his salary from $810,000 to $700,000. His contract allows for a bonus of up to 200 percent of his salary and automatically awards him restricted stock equal to 75 percent of his salary. At his request the compensation committee paid him no bonus for 1991 and reduced his award of restricted stock to 55 percent of his base in 1991 and 25 percent in 1992. Then the company made no announcement of what Reichert had done; it simply included the routine disclosure in the proxy statement.

THE VERY FIRST CITATION PRODUCT
TO GO UP IN THE AIR WASN'T A BUSINESS JET.

Before the first Citation ever rolled off the line, we built the first
service center dedicated exclusively to maintaining the aircraft.

Now, nearly 2,000 Citations later, there are Citation Service Centers
located 45 minutes apart throughout the contiguous United States, and
Authorized Citation Service Stations around the world.

When you own a Citation, we're here to take care of the aircraft so the
aircraft and you can do what you do best. Take care of business.

THE SENSIBLE CITATIONS

Cessna
A Textron Company

Chapter Five

STREAMLINING SERVICES

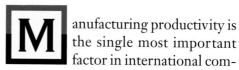anufacturing productivity is the single most important factor in international competitiveness. To a nation's overall progress and prosperity, however, productivity in services matters at least as much. As management guru Peter Drucker has written, "The single greatest challenge facing managers in the developed countries of the world is to raise the productivity of knowledge and service workers." Services is the area in which productivity performance has been dreadful. By most accounts service productivity has barely budged for two decades. Some economists calculate that the average white-collar worker's productivity has even declined since the early 1970s.

That defies logic because it implies that the hundreds of billions of dollars invested in computers has achieved nothing at all. Service productivity may look this bad because accurately measuring the quality of services is impossible. And many companies are using computers to do things they didn't do 20 or 30 years ago, so there's little basis for comparison. Whether those things are worth doing—whether they contribute to overall efficiency or output—is another matter. Managers, for example, typically have access to lots more information than in the past, much of which they don't need.

It does seem clear, though, that productivity in services has lagged significantly behind manufacturing. One reason is that most companies have used computers merely to mechanize manual tasks. In recent years, however, some service companies have found new ways to organize clerical workers and harness computers so that they are much more efficient. In the process, they are repeating a familiar pattern. Years ago, service industries and clerical departments within manufacturing companies adopted the same functional division of jobs introduced in manufacturing around the turn of the century. Now they are following manufacturers into the new world of JIT, work cells, and participative management. Says Waino Pihl, a managing partner of Andersen Consulting's banking practice: "I spend a lot of time reading manufacturing books and sending my people to manufacturing seminars so that we can apply what we have learned in manufacturing to financial services."

The most radical and effective technique for eliminating waste and boosting productivity in services is reengineering, the use of information technology to redesign business processes. What that means is thoroughly reassessing the "processes" a company is trying to accomplish instead of merely rethinking the procedures within a process. The technique is similar to JIT in the sense that it cuts wasteful procedures that reduce a company's output, but it entails a much deeper examination of existing practices.

Michael Hammer, a Cambridge, Massachusetts, consultant who invented the technique, hit upon reengineering while advising clients on how they could use new information technology to change the way they work. He argues that conventional business structures are too fragmented, in the sense that employees are grouped and managed along functional lines. That is, most employees are in departments divided according to the type of work a person does, such as accounting, distribution, purchasing, or design engineering. Under that system, managers and workers tend to put the narrow goals of departments ahead of the larger goals of the organization. Reengineering organizes those workers around the outcomes they are supposed to achieve together, not around individual tasks. "Reengineering is distinguished by two critical words, *process* and *radical*," says Hammer, a former computer science professor at MIT. "It is process-oriented rather than function-oriented. It is radical in the sense that it is not a technique for modest improvement but for radical change."

One of Hammer's favorite examples—Ford Motor's accounts

payable operation—illustrates what reengineering is about and what the technique can achieve. During a major cost-cutting push in the mid-1980s, Ford wanted to reduce the number of employees in accounts payable from 500 to 400. Then it learned that Mazda's accounts payable department consisted of just five people. After adjusting for the difference in company size, it was plain that Ford had five times as many people in accounts payable as it needed. "The Ford team knew better than to attribute the difference to calisthenics, company songs, or low interest rates," says Hammer. With that, Ford began to reengineer by examining just what accounts payable does, and why.

Under the old system, clerks in accounts payable matched up three documents: the purchase order, the receiving document, and the invoice. If 14 items of data on the three documents coincided, the department cut a check. If not, a clerk had to find out why and resolve the differences. Accounts payable spent most of its time on such mismatches. The problem, Ford concluded, was that the invoice was merely an unnecessary control mechanism in the process. What the company really wanted was to pay after it received goods whether an invoice had arrived or not.

Today Ford doesn't get invoices at all. Under the new system, purchasers enter orders in a central database. When a shipment arrives at a receiving dock, the receiving clerk checks a terminal to find an order that corresponds to the shipment. If he can't, he refuses the shipment. If he can, he accepts the shipment and enters the receipt transaction in the computer. The computer then compares just three items on the purchase order and the receipt record—the part number, the quantity of parts, and the supplier. If they match, the computer cuts a check and sends it to the supplier (although not necessarily right away). If they don't match, the computer kicks out the records for a clerk to reconcile. The change enabled Ford to cut its accounts payable head count by 75 percent while simplifying materials control and reducing errors in financial information.

Once a person learns how to define processes, reengineering becomes conceptually simple, but it is extremely difficult in practice. "It is easy to screw this up, and most people do," says Hammer. "It isn't difficult to come up with breakthrough ideas. The hard part is turning them into reality in a less than enthusiastic company. This entails enormous disruptions because it changes everything about the company—the culture, the organization, and how people are managed. Even though the results should be better for nearly everyone, most people are frightened by change, and the middle management tier is the group with the most to lose. It requires leadership from the very top."

One early innovator was Aid Association for Lutherans, a fraternal organization in Appleton, Wisconsin, and one of the largest U.S. life and health insurers. In 1987 AAL reorganized nearly 500 clerks and managers into self-directed work teams to process insurance claims more quickly and to provide better service to field agents and policyholders. The company established five geographic regions, each with a handful of teams of around 20 workers each. Each team now does all of the 167 tasks formerly split among three departments (life, health, and support services). A manager still oversees each team, but AAL was able to eliminate three layers of supervision. In its first year the change produced a 20 percent increase in labor productivity and slashed the average time to process a claim by 75 percent.

Banc One Mortgage, the Indianapolis-based lender, began a similar redesign of its application process in 1991. Banc One (a subsidiary of Banc One Corporation of Columbus, Ohio) had 400 mortgage originators and processors in 100 locations around the U.S. They operated in the industry's standard fashion, with one processor assigned to each originator. When a processor completed work on an application, it went to an underwriter for review and then to a loan closer. CEO Al Smith says his operation was growing so rapidly (from $1.7 billion of new mortgages in 1991 to more than $4.2 billion in 1992) that he had to find a faster and more efficient way to handle applications. "We had tried to grow by brute force," he says. "Now we are finding better ways."

In this case, the better way is a network of 15 regional production centers to replace the 100 offices. Each cell includes groups of processors—who work with all the originators in the geographic area instead of just one—along with underwriters and closers. Banc One also included a customer-service person in each cell to answer questions from applicants. The biggest change was ending the one-on-one relationship of originators and processors, which provided the immediate payoff of spreading the work more evenly. Under the old system, some processors had too little to do some of the time, while those working with the highest-producing originators were swamped.

Banc One has put all the applications on a local area network so that originators, processors, and underwriters can call up a file on their computer screens instead of hunting down the hard copy. The company is also equipping originators with notebook computers and modems so they can feed applications directly into the regional processing centers. Finally, Banc One has cross-trained members of the work cells so that processors can double as loan closers at month's end, when most mortgages are closed.

"The processors feel liberated," says Smith. "[The reorganization] reduced their stress and tension, and they now are able to divert endless calls from customers to the service rep." The new system required an adjustment for the originators, however. "They no longer have their own processors," adds Smith, "and there is a group that wants to have a slave at their beck and call." Still, the originators' discomfort pales before the improvements. The average processing time is down from 32 to 22 days, the number of applications sent to underwriters with all the paperwork complete is up from 78 to 92 percent, and Banc One handled a 153 percent increase in mortgage volume in the first half of 1992 with little increase in head count.

Waino Pihl, who helped design Banc One's regional processing centers, says banking is rife with opportunities for productivity improvement. The greatest potential is in the areas with the most people, notably back offices and retail branches. One of Pihl's clients is in the process of consolidating consumer-loan back-office operations from 10 affiliated banks into two centers. The centers will have work cells composed of everyone who works on loan processing and bad-debt collection, including attorneys, skip tracers, and the like. The change should enable the bank to cut its back-office staff by 40 to 50 percent and reduce data processing costs. "Accounting is another key area for change," Pihl says. "Banks have separate full-blown accounting departments for each country, for consumer lending, for credit cards, for commercial lending. This means thousands of unnecessary people."

Another example of service industry success with this kind of reorganization is Capital Holding, the Louisville life and health insurer. Irv Bailey began leading the change to participative management when he became president in 1987 (he moved up to chairman and CEO in the spring of 1988). "The company had a good track record, but it was a holding company with three businesses and no vision of how the company would develop," he says. "It was run the old way—people did not cooperate across functions or divisions." Bailey started by developing a corporate vision, a process that took

18 months and involved 40 people across the organization. The main message in the resulting statement is that all Capital Holding's employees will function as teams and focus on serving customers.

Bailey's team orientation is unusual given that he rose on the investment side of the company, where individual performance normally matters more than teamwork. "I ran investments, another executive ran annuities, and another ran guaranteed investment contracts," he says. "It was a classic marketing versus production split. Some of us had sales objectives, the rest profit-and-loss [objectives]." Bailey reorganized those specialties into one accumulation-and-investment group, or AIG. "We created an AIG school that everyone in the group attends so that everyone will focus on the same bottom-line objectives. Instead of measuring people on their individual objectives, we now measure [them] on the bottom line of the business." That orientation has given Capital Holding a big advantage over other insurers, Bailey says. "What makes us different is that we manage assets and liabilities together. Before we launch a product, we know what it will take to make money—both how to generate liabilities [that is, sell a particular type of annuity, guaranteed investment contract, or insurance policy] and manage the assets." In the old days, marketing and investment staff rarely communicated.

Capital Holding has invested considerable time and resources to indoctrinating managers in the potential of teamwork. Off-campus retreats are among Bailey's favorite techniques. One of the first was an Outward Bound-style exercise in North Carolina for more than 40 employees. Says Bailey: "The experience gives a vivid demonstration that you need more than one person to execute the solution to a problem. The biggest revelation is how many people can contribute."

Once Bailey had completed the reorganization of AIG, he set out to bring teamwork to the rest of Capital Holding. At a March 1989 meeting on Cape Cod, he assembled 40 people from all the divisions. Instructors put them through an exercise of making paper stars to demonstrate "the power of empowerment," as Bailey puts it. First the instructor, acting like a conventional supervisor, told the participants what to do. Then he had the people at each table collaborate to find other, simpler ways of making stars. "The improvement was exponential," Bailey says. The group became even more proficient when the teams at different tables began sharing ideas.

Bailey's next step was to form teams within the operating divisions. One of the first to implement the new system was the agency group in Durham, North Carolina. The agency group sells basic life and health coverage to middle- and lower-income households in the Southeast and mid-Atlantic states. Like most insurance company back offices, this one had been arranged according to function, such as underwriting, information checking, and pricing. "We didn't realize until we mapped the process that people were [sitting] in the wrong place," says Bailey. "No one had ever looked at the actual work flow."

The agency group moved people who work on different aspects of a policy application next to each other, so that work flows sequentially from desk to desk. Capital Holding also trained workers to do several jobs so they can pitch in to ease bottlenecks. The physical reorganization included open management offices with three walls instead of four, a change most headquarter executives didn't like at all. "We want to make the statement to employees that we are accessible to them and are here to work with them," Bailey says.

During the transition, the company held breakfasts to explain changes to nonofficers. Bailey says the program ran into the usual resistance from supervisors, who saw their jobs evaporating under a team regime. Some rank-and-file clerical workers were also cool to the new system. "There are people who won't change or can't change—who [want to be] told what to do," says Bailey. "If we were unionized, it would have been a hell of a problem." Bailey also encountered passive resistance at the executive level: "Some are advocates right away, others wait and see, and some view meetings as taking away from work no matter what the content of the meeting."

Capital Holding hasn't tried to measure the productivity gains, but they have plainly been enormous. The initial goal was to cut the time it takes to issue a policy from 15 to three days. The teams now process 30 percent of the applications in one day and the rest in two. The agency group has cut its administrative staff from 1,500 to 1,000—despite two acquisitions—and has a target of just 800 workers. "We told people that no performing employee would lose his or her job," says Bailey. "We have been able to move some to other areas of the company, but it's been tough."

In 1991 Capital Holding began testing similar cross-functional arrangements in its direct response group, which sells life, health, homeowners, and auto insurance via television commercials, direct mail, and telemarketing. First the company put all employees through a two-day seminar on teamwork. Now it is regrouping workers into "customer management" teams. The accident and health part of direct response, in Valley Forge, Pennsylvania, had been quintessentially conventional: supervisors made decisions and workers did the work, hewing to time standards for each task. Now cross-trained teams schedule their own vacations, order supplies, and so on. In less than a year, the number of applications that were immediately approved rose 13 percent, and the average response time on those requiring additional information dropped from 11.5 to 5.2 days.

Physical change came to headquarters as well when Capital Holding moved into new offices in 1992. Unlike the old offices, these have four walls. But the resemblance to the usual executive suite ends there. All the offices, including Bailey's, are 10 by 15 feet with glass fronts and identical furniture. Some executives chafed at the plebian accommodations. "But since I'm doing it," says Bailey, "they can't bitch a hell of a lot."

The company formalized its training and indoctrination of senior managers in 1991 by creating the Capital Holding Learning Institute. Together they read works such as *Genesis*, Plato's dialogues, and Martin Luther King Jr.'s "Letter From Birmingham Jail." They discuss their personal visions and the Capital Holding vision and then go through a day-and-a-half follow-up session several months later.

Bailey, a soft-spoken leader with a palpable enthusiasm for his company, says participative management and reengineering have been major forces behind Capital Holding's success. The company's stock has outperformed those of most other life insurers since he became CEO. As with other companies, however, the change has brought casualties among executives who could not adapt. "In a couple of instances, I asked senior managers to leave because they weren't in sync with our value system," Bailey says. "You send a strong message when you dismiss executives because they are not living the values." Bailey is quick to add that change must be a constant. "I don't know if we'll ever get where we want to go," he says.

How the U.S. responds to competitive challenges from abroad will have profound effects on living standards well into the next century. Virtually all economists agree that free trade makes all countries better off and that protectionism has the power to impoverish consumers everywhere. Unfortunately, the case for free trade often sounds abstract and has nowhere near as much political appeal as assertions that Americans are losing jobs to countries that refuse to compete on a "level playing field." In 1992, H. Ross Perot captured a higher percentage of the votes in a presidential election than any other third-party candidate since Theodore Roosevelt, and he ran on a blatantly protectionist platform. At the time of President Bush's trip to Tokyo, some in Congress were arguing that we should protect "American" jobs by putting quotas on the number of cars Toyota can build in Kentucky. Executives of the big three automakers and the United Auto Workers called on Bill Clinton before his inauguration to plead for more restrictions on Japanese imports. Calls for more tariffs and quotas are bound to continue, and politicians throughout the world may find them increasingly difficult to resist.

Competition, however, is always beneficial, whether it comes from a company across town or one across the ocean. It compels managers and workers to search more diligently for the innovations that reduce costs by boosting productivity, giving rise to faster improvements in real wages and living standards. In the years ahead, competition will force nearly all corporations, however reluctantly, to adopt many of the innovations described in this book. As they do, productivity should grow at a much faster rate than in the recent past. That is great news for the economy, but it could actually have a perverse effect on the political war over free trade.

That is because the productivity revolution will bring significant hardship for millions of workers whose jobs will be eliminated by reengineering and JIT manufacturing. And this time, the displaced will not be the shop-floor workers who have historically been the primary victims of labor-saving innovations. They will be middle managers, supervisors, and office workers—people who have suffered when their employers came on hard times but who previously had little to fear from the word productivity. The greatest inefficiencies in U.S. business are in support functions, not in direct manufacturing, and it is support workers whose jobs will be lost. Indeed, production workers in JIT factories have learned that productivity does not threaten but actually preserves their jobs by lowering costs and keeping them competitive. That cannot be said for support personnel and middle managers.

Eliminating all those jobs will be a boon to the economy as a whole. People, like minerals in the ground, are a natural resource. If they can be freed from doing things that don't need to be done, they will be available to produce goods and services that aren't being produced now, which will raise national income and living standards. That is something Luddites have never understood. The adjustment to new, more efficient ways of operating, however, will cause financial and emotional hardship for the millions of people forced to find new jobs, many of which will initially pay less than those lost. As a result, broad-based restructuring is bound to bring forth political charges that heartless executives are sacrificing employees in a wrongheaded response to the competitiveness problem.

One of the ironies of the productivity revolution is that participative management requires chief executives to show more heart by treating all subordinates with more respect and deference while also being heartless in the pursuit of more efficient ways of organizing businesses. But chief executives have no choice other than to be heartless in their pursuit of productivity. Those who refuse to take on the hard work of reshaping their corporate cultures will eventually find that their companies can no longer compete with domestic or foreign rivals. Letting a company fail by refusing to change is the most heartless course of all.

EVERY 22 SECONDS, SOMETHING QUITE UNEVENTFUL
HAPPENS SOMEWHERE IN THE WORLD.

A Citation takes off or lands safely every 22 seconds. The aircraft's safety record is even more remarkable considering there are nearly 2,000 of them in the world's largest fleet of business jets.

In aviation, the Collier Trophy is the highest tribute to excellence. The trophy was created in 1911, but 75 years went by before it was given to honor a business aircraft company.

The Citation's unmatched safety record is why that company is Cessna.

THE SENSIBLE CITATIONS

Cessna
A Textron Company

ADDITIONAL COPIES

To order additional copies of *Found Money*
for friends or colleagues, please write to
The Chief Executive Press, Whittle Books,
333 Main St., Knoxville, Tenn. 37902.
Please include the recipient's name, mailing
address, and, where applicable, title,
company name, and type of business.

For a single copy, please enclose a check
for $13.95, plus $3.50 postage and
handling, payable to The Chief Executive
Press. Discounts are available for orders of 10
or more books. If you wish to order by
phone, call 800-284-1956.

Also available, at the same price,
are the previous books from
The Chief Executive Press:
Getting the Job Done by Kenneth L. Adelman,
What Are You Worth? by Graef S. Crystal,
and *Pressure Points* by Robert W. Lear.

Please allow two weeks for delivery.
Tennessee residents must add 8¼ percent sales tax.